# INTO THE NEEDLE'S EYE

## *Becoming Poor and Hopeful Under the Care of a Gracious God*

### WILLIAM E. REISER, S.J.

AVE MARIA PRESS
Notre Dame, Indiana

*Imprimi Potest:*
Very Rev. Edward M. O'Flaherty, S.J.
Provincial, Society of Jesus of New England

———————————————————————————

©1984 by Ave Maria Press, Notre Dame, Indiana 46556.

International Standard Book Number:   0-87793-305-7 (Cloth)
0-87793-306-5 (Paper)

Library of Congress Catalog Card Number:   83-72741

Printed and bound in the United States of America.

*Cover and text design:* Elizabeth French

# Contents

*T*hen Jesus said to his disciples, "I tell you the truth, it is hard for a rich man to enter the kingdom of heaven. Again I tell you, it is easier for a camel to go through the eye of a needle than for a rich man to enter the kingdom of God." When the disciples heard this, they were greatly astonished and asked, "Who then can be saved?" Jesus looked at them and said, "With man this is impossible, but with God all things are possible."

*Matthew 19:23-26*

# Introduction

The snake charmer had just finished tying his basket. Three times he had circled the grounds of the mission, and each time he detected the scent of a cobra. He didn't see the snake, but he could smell it. Examining the ground closely and poking at the rat holes with his staff, he would coax the snake's attention by chanting a string of nonsense phrases. After a few moments the earth would flicker, two shades of brown rubbing past each other. Quick and alert as a mongoose, he would land his staff across a snake as it rustled through the tall grass of the rice field. A young boy carried the straw basket into which the charmer deposited each snake and then cautiously secured the cover before the creatures could coil and spread their hoods. The first two cobras measured about three feet apiece, but the last one was nearly five feet long! Since snakes usually travel in pairs, we returned to the house somewhat alarmed about where the mate of the five-footer might be hiding.

Most days on the mission did not provide the remarkable material for such a good story. Even in Asia, life assumes its necessary ordinariness and routine. Yet, for the eyes of a Westerner, Asia tends to throw the simple features of daily life into memorable relief. The brilliant, almost iridescent green of rice paddies lit by the sun after a monsoon shower, barefooted children holding hands and singing under a coconut tree, hundreds of tiny shops along mud roads baked by the sun, the dust churned up by buses and lorries rattling over potholes and ditches, flies and scrawny dogs, faces and limbs belonging to the weary, the landless, and the crippled: Every day offers material for another sort of story, stories about life and death, faith and hope. The bulging trains of India seem to be telling you that all of humanity, traveling together on a journey which no one relishes, will soon burst its seams and derail.

Asia has tasted and enjoyed many of the fruits of Western culture. Coca-Cola, Mobil, Sheraton, Chase-Manhattan . . . these are a few of the multinational code names for progress that one expects to find in cities like Hong Kong, Singapore, and Bangkok. But you can buy a cassette recording of Willie Nelson or John Denver, or pick up a jar of Skippy peanut butter from a market shelf, at a bazaar in central Java.

Still, Asia shows its true face in its villages, its teeming populations, its ancient cultures and religions, its architecture and burial customs, its rice and curries, its teas and spices, its geographical contrasts, its climate. These are the things which have fascinated Westerners ever since Marco Polo, that medieval merchant from Venice, told of his journeys through the kingdom of the Great Khan. But Asia is no more mysterious than any other place; it is merely different. The jumble of tones and sounds which comprise an Oriental language, together with the lines and squiggles that make up its alphabet, can be deciphered to reveal the basic grammar of human life no matter where in the Far East one lands. Asian societies have their share of social, political, economic and administrative problems. Original sin plagues the Asian condition just as much as it affects ours. Countless numbers of people live on the margin of survival because of corrupt government officials and the greed of wealthy landlords. The resignation on the faces of a group of villagers who had been swindled out of their rice harvest left me an unforgettable image for the cry of the poor.

The most visible traits of Asian life may well be poverty and religion, two features which cannot fail to alert a Christian to possibilities for God's presence in the world. Jesus showed a preference for the company of poor people, and he was zealous about explaining to them how and where they should search for the kingdom of God. Whether the temple is Hindu or Buddhist, whether the building is a Christian church or a Muslim mosque, whenever you see poor people entering it, you know that God must be nearby. And yet, would Jesus have looked like a foreigner if he had journeyed to Asia? Is Christianity so tied to Europe and the Americas that our churches will always look a bit incongruous on Oriental soil? How does one dare to be Christian while standing under the powerful gaze of the Buddha?

There was an afternoon downpour after the snakes left, and a rainbow had anchored itself to both ends of the horizon. Like a magnificent arch colored with hope and promise, it drew together each fold in the earth—the fields, the mud houses, the families, the banana trees, the water buffalo—until evening drew on and the stars took hold of the sky. If God had been anywhere on earth at that moment, he was certainly there, stepping through a small village in northern India. From the rooftop overlooking the mission, my experience of the last several months started to crystalize. Our encounter with God, India seemed to say, revolves around two reference points: the experience of poverty and the power of hope. Being poor is part of the human condition. Even wealthy foreigners are poor, perhaps all the more so because they neither see their poverty easily nor accept it honestly. God cannot touch them until they see how poor they really are, a fact which begins showing itself when they find themselves for the first time in a situation where money is no longer available to alleviate human misery. One has to learn how to follow the Jesus who has neither money nor power.

Yet there is hope. Perhaps nothing symbolizes modern times so frightfully and accurately as the atom. It stands for the privatization of life, the illusion of limitless energy and power, and the dizzy moral relativism so typical of Western societies. But Asia forces one to notice the immense solidarity of the human race, the many links which draw and keep people together in their shared experience of life and death. There is no privacy among the poor, no room to withdraw from the daily reminders of the world's inefficiency, its

breath, and its decay. Poverty is not a solitary, atomic matter; but then, neither is one's relationship with God. For
God draws people out of their isolation and into life. The
people whom Jesus healed returned to their villages and
families. God leads people to trust that their dreams are
precious to him and that his designs for the human race are
still workable. He offers us his own vision and dream, and
throws in a rainbow every now and then, in order that we
might see and understand the hope in which we are being
created, the common destiny of the human family.

Many Third-World scenes look like they might have
slipped from the pages of the gospels, an impression that
makes the life of Jesus seem curiously contemporary even in
Asia. One afternoon in Indonesia an ancient-looking
woman (she was probably no more than 50 years old)
stopped at a small, dusty roadside shop. The skin of her face
and arms, dried and wrinkled from the tropical sun, held to
her bones like paper glued to the bark of an old tree. When
she returned to the narrow lane her cheeks were puffed out
with a great mouthful of tobacco that stuck through her
lips. By bending forward to a right angle, she turned her
back into a platform on which she balanced a basket loaded
with firewood. I was about five or six paces ahead of her
when a large turkey suddenly appeared and strutted across
the road. It paused, made a few clucking sounds, relieved
itself right there in front of me, made several more sounds
which I interpreted as sighs of relief, and vanished behind a
hedge. The old woman let loose a string of cackles. Turning
toward the new noises, I watched the spread of a wide,
toothless grin. I presumed that she was expressing amuse-
ment at my astonishment over the turkey, and we laughed
together. *Salamat pagi* means "good morning." It was one
of the two or three phrases I knew, so I used it to greet her
through a grin of my own. That confused her. She probably
figured that I couldn't tell the time of day.

At first, the contrast between the turkey's bearing, its handsome tail feathers, and its careless manners before a foreign visitor, intimated a fable; I began to feel like Aesop. The real story, however, would have to involve me and the old woman with the tobacco-pouch jowls, whose chortling put me at ease and carried a reminder that the needs of nature do not take a holiday just because an American is passing through the neighborhood. Not a fable, but a parable was brewing; I gradually imagined myself more like an evangelist: The kingdom of God might be compared to an old Javanese woman who made an American stranger feel at home.

One reason for my traveling to Asia was to learn about the other world religions and to observe how successfully the gospel had taken root in Eastern cultures. I had also hoped to discover that the people of Asia were bringing new flavor to their Christian faith and finding fresh approaches to reading the gospel. The incident from that afternoon had underlined the fact that noble ideas, even ideas about God and his angels, never outgrow their down-to-earth relatives, the images and experiences of daily life. Jesus' parables—his homespun examples about threadbare garments, new wine, finding a sack of money in a vacant lot, fruitless trees, lost coins, and so on—reveal how well he realized that the things of earth are not beneath the dignity of ideas about the kingdom of God. God was not too finely dressed to walk through the towns and villages of Palestine. Neither was God going to be a stranger to the neighborhoods and rice paddies of Asia. Perhaps that's why Asian theologian Kosuke Koyama coined the phrase "waterbuffalo theology."

What went on behind the scenes of Jesus' imagination? How was he able to notice so many connections between everyday concerns and happenings, and the kingdom of God? The kingdom of heaven, for Jesus, was like so many things: like a man who sowed good seed in his garden, like yeast, like buried treasure, like mustard seed, like fishing nets, like an ambitious merchant, like the homecoming of a runaway son, and so on. Each detail in the life he saw unfolding around him could trigger a reflection about the kingdom, about God's rule in the world. On what basis did Jesus derive his confidence to assure the crowds that followed him not to worry about where they would get their next meal, or about their clothes, or about settling scores with their oppressors? Indeed, Jesus had stiff words for the rich and powerful, but his message to the poor sounds so innocent, maybe even naive. How did he manage to get away with the Sermon on the Mount? Jesus had seen withered hands, blinded eyes, leprous stumps, foaming epileptics, dead children, weeping fathers, terrified women. Beggars had stretched open hands toward him, and he had heard the tragic news stories of his day—people being killed by falling towers or ambushed by tyrants. No, Jesus was hardly naive; his life had not been sheltered against touching misfortune, and the gospels never portray him trying to defend his Father against the problem of evil. But this means that Jesus was absolutely convinced of his message. Jesus looked the poor and sorrowing straight in the eye and said, "You are blessed!" Jesus' confidence rested on his experience of God, and many people found themselves believing Jesus.

The God to whom Jesus prayed was one who cared, who loved, who accepted all, no matter what they had done. God was the Father, and all people, not just princes and priests, could talk with God as daughters and sons. Unless Jesus had become familiar with God in this way from his own prayer, his own meditation upon scripture, and his intuitions about life, we would never be able to comprehend the basis of his teaching. There would be no way to penetrate his vision of life.

Most Christians feel comfortable with the teachings of Jesus. His teachings seem right to us and fit our expectations of what God should be like even when we don't live out that teaching faithfully in every detail. We trust Jesus' religious intuitions. But left to our own devices, we would probably not have arrived at the same understanding of God which Jesus reached. There is no cause for jealousy or self-reproach in this. We have no reason to be upset because Jesus knew God more intimately than we do, and there is no point in belittling ourselves for the spiritual dullness which makes us less alert to the numerous signs of God's presence in everyday life. Nevertheless, we can hope that our experience of God will grow as much like Jesus' experience as God will allow. "No one can have any knowledge of God unless God teaches him," wrote the second-century bishop, St. Irenaeus. And so we can pray to know God as Jesus knew him. For Christians, knowing God will forever be bound up with knowing Jesus. It will mean sharing in the same Spirit which filled and guided Jesus, leading him to see the world as only a son of God could see it. As Paul explained to the Romans, "those who are led by the Spirit of God are sons of God," and "the Spirit himself testifies with our spirit that we are God's children" (Rom 8:14, 16). This text illumines the words of Isaiah: "All your sons will be taught by the Lord, and great will be your children's peace" (Is 54:13).

Religion and life did not become two separate spheres for Jesus. He did not appeal to the images and experiences of daily living in order to entice people into the tent of religion. Religion was one of life's great possibilities; it might break through at any moment, like kernels opening to the soil's moisture or dough rising with the action of yeast. With so many fishermen around him, no one could accuse Jesus of making religion into a domestic affair of pious women. The sturdiness of his words and the ruggedness of his images—cornerstones, yoked oxen, hauls of fish and skins of wine, rowing and plowing, hammers and crossbeams—make it clear that Jesus viewed religion within the fabric of everyone's life, women and men alike. Religion claims the whole of life for itself: Nothing is foreign to the meaning of the kingdom, everything manifests the urgency of God's will.

For some time, I have been thinking about the question of how the privileged Christian of today finds hope for entering the kingdom of God. Since 1972, I made my way to the Far East six times, to touch in whatever way I could the suffering and poverty one associates with places like Calcutta and Bangladesh. The opportunity for so much travel already marks me as among the affluent, I know. But the need to see for myself the miserable conditions which I had been hearing and reading about for so long was strong. In some way, at stake was the way I conceived the possibility of my own salvation. How do we justify our way of life to ourselves, how do we even kneel down to pray, in view of the fact that whenever we sit down to eat, millions of our fellow human beings—people with memories, feelings, and minds—have to face the parched lands and barren fields that once fed them? What words do we say to God when so many of our sisters and brothers are fleeing from lands burned by war, leaving their crops, their homes, and their histories behind, or are watching helplessly as their children's limbs shrivel with hunger and thirst? On the one hand, no Western Christian can live out the Good News while shouldering heavy feelings of guilt about his or her comfort and safety. But, on the other hand, one cannot ignore the voices and faces underlining the solidarity in flesh and blood, in mind and soul, which binds all the nations together as God's people.

The pages that follow try to tell a brief and often personal account of how one Christian has attempted to make sense of what he has seen in some of the world's hunger and poverty, and to come to terms with what he observed in the foreign religions that often appear to tower over one's own faith. Christians are comparatively few in Asia, where the gospel frequently competes with powerful ascetic and contemplative traditions. *Being religious, it seems to me, involves becoming poor and hopeful under the caring eye of a gracious God.* That, in a nutshell, is my main idea. Turning poor means listening respectfully and openly to the word of God which may speak to us from within another religious tradition. Turning poor means acknowledging that each and every one of us really does belong to the whole human family. Turning poor means becoming compassionate and learning how to dispossess our resentments and anger. Turning poor means entering the solitary chamber of one's own heart and confronting the stark, dreary spaces of one's inner poverty. With religious pilgrims throughout the ages, turning poor requires laying aside those cherished attachments that cannot be carried on the steeper roads of life's journey. Turning poor means letting go of self for the love of God, as Jesus let go of his self for love of us.

The solution, then, to how one is to be saved is rather simple; a child can grasp it, the "little ones" of this world. But the application of the gospel to any particular life has a way of growing terribly entangled with the salvation of others, friends and strangers alike. The gospel does not provide a program for moving the nuts and bolts of the world's political and economic systems. Many times I have wished that I held in my hands the resources of the rich nations, but all of that wealth and power will not convert evil, crooked minds toward justice—not even in the Third World. Greed among the poor is ugly, but it is understandable. Avarice among the rich and powerfully stationed, however, is like a spreading cancer that chews away at the face of the world. Thus there are the political, social, and historical realities that define the time and place in which each generation must figure out how to live the gospel. It is deceptively easy to determine what message should be preached to the rich: Moral outrage over injustice leads directly into the rhetoric of prophetic denunciation. But most of us are not poor enough to be prophets, a point I shall develop later. However, what shall we say to those who are poor? Is it possible for us to communicate to the poor and victimized people of this world, without blushing in embarrassment, that God cares for them, if at the same time we are wrestling with doubts about God's ability to demonstrate that care? Jesus managed because he really believed and loved God, like a son.

If my ideas appear disconnected as the book unfolds, I beg the reader's patience. There are many gaps in my experience. Indeed, the stitching of faith often runs unevenly, unfinished. Sometimes you feel for weeks and months that you have been crawling through a needle's eye, and then one day you catch a glimpse of the patchwork of divine grace over your life and tell yourself that, if camels can make it, you should hope to do the same. The first chapter gives the full account of a little story I told on a page in *America* magazine several summers ago. In that chapter I have tried to relate some of the doubts, the questions, the challenges and the discoveries a Christian might experience in encountering another world religion up close. The secret of escaping the spell cast by another religion lies in letting go of one's habitual way of looking at Jesus and trusting the gospel's power to hold its own in the religious arena. We have to turn poor in matters religious, letting go of "God" for God's sake, as medieval mystic Meister Eckhart would say.

In the second chapter I have explored the connection between being truthful and being poor. One of the stumbling blocks to living in the truth is our tendency to cling to everything except God for security (which seems fairly obvious), but we have to learn to surrender any attempt to use truth as if truth were a tool and we were its masters. When you think about it, the truth has us; truth (in a Christian understanding of truth) is God himself. There is a power in truth. The power of truth consists in its ability to lay us

14

bare, to open us and expose our inner cravings, fantasies and confusion. When truth uncovers us, we realize how empty and poor we really are.

The third chapter reworks an article which appeared in *Review for Religious.* That chapter develops a model of Christian living. I believe that all Christians are asked to identify with the world with which Jesus identified when he walked among the poor, sat at table with sinners, touched the diseased and handicapped, or consoled those who had lost heart. We need to be taught, however, that we are the ones with whom Jesus identified. We carry the world inside of us, with its sin, its grief, its poverty, its loneliness, its failure. Jesus became poor for our sake, but we do not empty ourselves and thus become poor for the world's sake, for none of us is rich to start with. We are all poor; in acknowledging this condition we make it possible for Jesus to share his riches with us.

The fourth chapter considers the urge to travel, for traveling is a metaphor of life itself. The seasoned traveler journeys more like a pilgrim than a tourist, and being a pilgrim calls for a genuine simplicity in one's living and thinking. The rich young man who appears in the tenth chapter of Mark's gospel leaves the way on which Jesus is journeying because he would not part with his wealth, while the blind beggar jumped to his feet when Jesus called him and threw aside his tattered cloak. Bartimaeus was no longer blind; he was free, and so he followed Jesus "along the way."

The fifth chapter took its initial shape on the pages of *Spirituality Today.* In that chapter I try my hand at a little theological speculation. What if God were to save all human beings—the good and the bad alike—because of the patient endurance, the prayer and the compassion of a few who in every age keep asking God to forgive those who have done them wrong? What if compassion were the highest realization of grace in us? What if the victory of a few who became champions of compassion were sufficient for rescuing the whole of our earthly city from eternal disaster? Then I think we would have to say that God is moved more by the holiness of a few than by the offenses of the many. We would be saying that compassion means turning poor, letting go of resentments, hatred, mistrust, and all preoccupation about reward for virtue and punishment for the wicked. Chapter Five would win, I like to think, an approving nod from the Buddha.

The underlying relationship among the chapters is the theme that being religious involves turning poor. But the chapters do not systematically build on one another, and so I have placed interludes between the chapters in order to invite a moment of pause, reflection, and transition. The book's final chapter serves as an epilogue where I have pulled together a number of loose ends in my reflection about being religious. Throughout the book scriptural quotations are taken from the New International Version of the Bible.

One day some orphans grabbed my hand and tugged me toward a guava tree which belonged to the local convent. The fruit was too high for the children to pick, and I was being enlisted to pull the branches within reach. The sisters also had a taste for guava, but I had become a not-so-unwilling partner to the children's scheme. We smiled like conspirators when the sisters came running with brooms and rakes to chase us away. That scene—the orphans, their smiles, the pieces of fruit, the stretching of hands, the chase—assembled many of the elements of poverty and hopefulness one observes on the faces of children in the Third World. That we in the developed countries should never forget how their future is coming to be part of ours is the most appropriate prayer I can make.

WILLIAM REISER, S.J.
*St. Xavier's School at Godavari*
*Kathmandu*

# 1

## The Buddha's Ears

This, O King, is an immediate fruit of the life of a recluse, and higher and sweeter than the last. With his heart thus serene, made pure, transparent, cultured, devoid of evil, supple, ready to act, firm and imperturbable, he applies and bends down his mind to the Heavenly Ear. With the clear Heavenly Ear surpassing the ear of men he hears sounds both human and celestial, whether far or near.

*Dialogues of the Buddha*

When St. Francis Xavier set sail for the Indies on April 7, 1541, a vigorous 35 years old, he carried in his heart both a glowing love for Christ and the 16th-century conviction that many heathen souls were perishing because they had not heard the truth of the gospel and received baptism. By the time Thomas Merton made his journey to the Far East in October, 1968, with the hope of making contact with Buddhist monasticism and observing some of it firsthand, the conception of Christian missionary activity had undergone almost revolutionary change. In fact, some Christians had become so reticent about the truth claims of their faith in the years following the Second Vatican Council that enthusiasm like Xavier's would have appeared to them evangelically embarrassing. For others, the gospel's apostolic drive was neutralized by a fear that the other world religions might be adequate paths to salvation after all. Had Christians been misled? It doesn't seem fair for God to have been present all along in the non-Christian religions while allowing us Christians to think that we had cornered the market in matters of religious truth.

Judging from some of the diaries and records they left us, the missionaries of the 16th and 17th centuries often encountered savagery and barbarism at its worst. As missioners like Patrick, Columban, and Boniface had already discovered, evangelizing people and civilizing them frequently went hand in hand. The missioner's first impression of Hinduism in 16th-century India, or of Taoism in 17th-century China, might have been similar to a traveler's impression of Christianity at the onset of the Dark Ages.

But missionaries to Asia had less success than the monks and missioners who evangelized Europe, perhaps because Asia had known some highly developed forms of civilization in an age when Europe was still the playground of barbarian tribes. In the Far East, missioners not only evangelized; they also Westernized and Europeanized, although there were some notable exceptions. The story of Mateo Ricci tells the exciting but sad adventure of a missionary to China whose wonderful experiment in adapting Christianity to an Eastern culture was terminated by a church more European than Catholic. The missionary had to sail with merchants and soldiers aboard royal fleets; greed, conquest, and colonial rule often proved to be the tares which choked his efforts. It was practically inevitable that ancient, venerable cultures which had lapsed into disarray would soon resist the Christian message.

However, a religion cannot be evaluated solely on the basis of the culture in which one finds it, since it is not religion's fault that a society or even an entire civilization starts to decay. Atrophy sets in only when people no longer respond to the moral and spiritual claims which their religion makes upon them. Nevertheless, the world religions show remarkable powers of self-purification and rejuvenation. And if a religion is so intertwined with a culture that people would be unable to change their religion without adopting a new cultural identity (a problem in many parts of Asia), then the Christian apostle will have to walk a theological tightrope.

People cannot be expected to renounce their cultural backgrounds. Yet the Christian story requires, at least for a while, that people turn their eyes from their own history and culture in order to notice what God has said to the world in Jesus, the man from Nazareth in Galilee, who lived nearly 2,000 years ago. The problem of expressing the gospel message in ways that people of other cultures will understand can be overcome. Missionaries of the past were quite adept at learning native languages and compiling dictionaries; missioners of today are watching local churches and home-grown thinkers move beyond the stage of learning languages into the stage of developing ideas, images, and idioms which express the religious spirit of their culture. But we have no formula at present that allows someone to remain both Hindu and Christian, or Christian and Buddhist. Even so, Christians today are seeking out other religious believers. Christians realize that truth, since it comes from God, should never be feared; and openness to God comes from being a pilgrim people.

Perhaps this explains the appearance of a Trappist like Thomas Merton, or of the Benedictines' Bede Griffiths and Swami Abhishiktananda. In traveling to the Orient, Merton drew many Christian eyes eastward with him. Some people were puzzled, some were distressed, but others were thrilled at Merton's needing to meet, to understand, and prayerfully to join those seeking for enlightenment and peace in the contemplative silence of Eastern monasteries. Christian religious life, Merton seemed to be revealing, had freed itself of those triumphalistic pretensions which so offended non-Western cultures and turned them away from the real message of Jesus. The two Benedictines bridged the great spiritual worlds of Christianity and Hinduism. Bede Griffiths set up a Christian community in India modeled on the Hindu ashram, and Abhishiktananda opened himself to an experience of Hindu spirituality which led him to settle eventually in the Himalayas as a hermit, just like a genuine Indian holy man. Letting their souls draw deeply from new cultural and spiritual soil, these Christian monks from the West have demonstrated what turning poor for the sake of the kingdom can mean today.

There are two personal stories which I want to relate, for they illustrate the feelings a Christian might experience when closely exposed to another world religion.

In Thailand it is customary for young men to spend a year apprenticed to a monastery where they will learn some of the Buddhist teaching and tradition. Since being Thai amounts to being Buddhist, this custom also acquaints the young men with a large part of their cultural heritage. Early in the morning and again late in the afternoon, with heads shaved, sandals on their feet, wearing the saffron robe of a monk and carrying the monk's traditional brass bowl, they pour out of temple compounds and walk the streets to beg for food, just as Buddhist monks have been doing for 2,500 years. During the middle of the day, the young men can be seen milling around the grounds of their monasteries. Some may be reading or chatting, or attending a class conducted by one of the senior monks, while others might be playing Ping-Pong or enticing an English-speaking tourist into conversation. Many of the monks want to improve their English; a few have hopes of one day traveling abroad. To a tourist, the young monks might seem to behave like flies around a piece of fruit—not always the most edifying displays of Buddhism at its best.

Three or four of them had latched onto me while I was waiting for a bus; they had just finished their round of begging for their breakfast. After exhausting the stock questions about where I had come from, what my profession was, how much money I earned, and how long I intended to stay in Bangkok, one of them advised me that the monks in the various monasteries around the city were not equally serious about being monks. A glance from one of his companions indicated that the remark was inappropriate in the hearing of a foreigner. It was evident to me that many of the city's temples had become tourist attractions, with their gold statues of the Buddha, their marble floors and walls, and the rough stone carvings which adorned the alcoves and outside stupas. In one of the temples, I had spied the abbot seated high on two or three crimson cushions while several young monks dashed around him with flashbulbs and cameras. Outside, a tour guide had been describing in broken English the Buddhist legends depicted in the statuary and carvings.

"How serious are they about their faith?" I was wondering as the companions left me to my bus. Religion can be so identified with a culture that the religion loses vitality and becomes merely a cultural expression of a colorful but harmless part of the past. St. Peter's in Rome or the Church of the Holy Sepulchre in Jerusalem may not be the most outstanding sites of Christian devotion, and I could recall many Christians who wouldn't belong to any other religion because being an American normally meant being Christian too. Often that's where the matter ended, in a name. And I remembered the monk at the shrine on Calvary who insisted I purchase and light a candle, which he promptly extinguished and resold as soon as I dropped out of sight.

The bus wound its way through the noise and traffic of the morning rush hour, stopping, starting, swerving to avoid hitting a few stalled taxis, crawling its way through some pineapples and mangosteens which had spilled in a collision between a rickshaw and a fruit cart. The bus then turned down a spacious avenue. My ears relaxed and my eyes now roamed more freely. I happened to look toward the driver and noticed him as he bowed his head. He had nodded just as we passed a temple. Several blocks further, another temple came into view. I saw it in time to observe four or five of the passengers bowing their heads too. That

21

was my signal. I jumped from the bus and started walking back toward the temple.

From inside the gate and across a courtyard, a voice from a loudspeaker was delivering a sermon. Thirty or 40 people were sitting on blankets or steps, looking toward an elderly monk who sat cross-legged in front of a microphone and read his message. Here and there people were standing in front of a Buddha image, moving their lips, raising joined hands toward their foreheads, and bowing low. It was the time of the annual rains-retreat, the Buddhist Lenten season, I was told. Gradually I made my way to a corner of the yard where I might observe the goings-on unnoticed. But no one seemed to mind my being there. In fact, several motioned to me with a smile to join them on their blankets.

Behind the old monk, on a great stone platform, there was a particularly large and impressive Buddha image. A wide saffron stole had been draped across its shoulder. With its solemn, contemplative face, its long ears symbolizing wisdom, its crossed legs and open palms, the statue fascinated me. It suggested someone in touch with the stillness of God. Over the years, faithful pilgrims had placed so many strips of gold leaf over the bronze that the statue seemed to be made of gold. There was nothing noisy and busy about this service I had stumbled into; everything had been set at ease by the silent peace represented in the Buddha statue.

Suddenly I remembered that I was a Christian, that the monk did not belong to my tradition, that the statue was not one of my saints, the sacred text not one out of my Bible, and the Lenten season was not recalling the life of Jesus. To make matters worse, the sudden recollection caught me in the middle of a personally unflattering thought. "Could it be," I had been wondering, "that the Buddha's experience of God ran deeper than Jesus' experience?" Once the question had slipped out, however unconscious or unintended it was, my insides blushed with shame. I whispered a quick prayer

22

of apology and turned to see if anyone had noticed my sudden discomfort. And then there was the Buddha's stare! Such a question, it seemed to say, reveals that you have not yet experienced God deeply, because those who do know God have transcended the need to compare their experience with that of someone else.

That brief confrontation with the Buddha brought to light some lingering feelings of doubt about the adequacy of my own spiritual life. Had I failed to grasp important elements of the Christian religious experience? Was I threatened by the spiritual achievements of people outside my religious tradition? The meeting also left me with great respect for the God-presence within Buddhism. Had there been no God-presence in that temple, I would have gone home undisturbed.

The disturbance lingered until, on a visit to India several years later, someone suggested seeing Bodh-Gaya, one of the world's holy places. The city of Gaya lies a half-day's train ride from the northern Indian city of Patna and the great Ganges River. On the outskirts of Gaya, at a place now called Bodh-Gaya, the Buddha received his enlightenment some five centuries before the birth of Christ.

July is a miserably hot and steamy month of the Indian monsoon season. The dark hills around Gaya drink up the sun during the day and release their stored heat during the night, turning the air into an insect paradise. But in the excitement of being so near to one of the world's great religious sites, I soon forgot about the heat and mosquitoes, and hired a taxi-scooter for the few miles further to Bodh-Gaya.

With visitors and pilgrims from all over India and other countries in Asia, Bodh-Gaya took on the carnival air of an Oriental bazaar. It covers a large area, sporting Buddhist temples that have been built and sponsored by many Asian countries where Buddhism remains strong—Burma, Korea, Japan, Thailand, China, Nepal, and of course India itself.

23

Each temple reflected its own brand of Buddhism and architectural style. The central temple appeared much older than it actually was. A few beggars waited outside the gate to provide pilgrims with an opportunity to practice compassion. Inside the gate, following Oriental custom, I left my sandals on the steps and walked down into the compound's gardens, toward the temple. Behind the building there stands (so I was told) a third-generation bo tree, a descendant of the original tree where the Buddha sat in meditation ages ago. The tree is enormous. Its trunk might measure 25 feet around and its broad leaves are higher than a man's reach.

According to legend, the Buddha one day seated himself under the tree, meditating. After six hours, he was enlightened with the first of the fourfold Noble Truths, the truth about pain and suffering. On receiving this enlightenment, he moved 90 degrees and faced a different direction. Again he meditated until, after six hours, he received the second of the fourfold Noble Truths, the truth about craving or desire, which is the cause of all suffering. Then six hours later, facing a new direction, he came to understand the third Noble Truth about how to overcome suffering. Finally, in the last quarter of the day, the Buddha was enlightened with the fourth Noble Truth, the path which leads to all truth and blessedness.

I knew the legend. For the sake of doing something, I decided to re-enact a bit of the story by sitting beneath the bo tree for 60 minutes, changing directions each quarter of an hour, to find out if the process of enlightenment could be telescoped. Nothing happened. As the compound filled with tourists and pilgrims, it seemed wiser to visit a few of the less-frequented temples. The Thai-style temple was a ten-minute walk down a gravel road, and I began recalling the great bronze statue which had challenged me to re-examine my understanding of God.

The building was spacious and empty. Stepping out of my sandals, I immediately liked the coolness of the polished marble floor. After a few moments of studying the many Buddha images lining the walls, I settled cross-legged on the floor and opened a pocket New Testament to the gospel of Luke. Why Luke? I'm not altogether sure, but the Jesus in John seemed too obvious for the occasion, the Jesus in Matthew too Jewish, and the Jesus in Mark too quick and single-minded. My attention fell upon a text, and I started whispering the verses slowly; the words sounded strange in the Asian setting, as if they had been stolen from the churches and chapels where they belonged. "Had anyone done this sort of thing before—read from the gospel of Luke in the middle of Bodh-Gaya?" The question helped me taste the adventure of the moment.

Into the second chapter. "In those days Caesar Augustus issued a decree . . ." Someone seemed to be listening to me, so I turned to see who had entered the temple. No one was there. My stomach jumped, but I continued reading. "Do not be afraid—I bring you news of great joy . . ." Another pause. Someone *was* listening. I stood up and cautiously circled the building to find out if the new visitor was squatting behind a pillar or had ducked into a corner, but there was no one else. Returning to my place a little nervously, I read further:

> that will be for all the people. Today in the town of David a savior has been born to you; he is Christ the Lord (Lk 2:1-11).

The alarm came back stronger than ever; there could be no mistake, *someone* was listening. And glancing up, I caught the Buddha's expression; it was the Buddha who was listening! The long-eared Buddha images which sat along the walls, and the large statue in front of me, had stirred from centuries-long contemplation and turned their heads to hear the words being whispered in their temple. I stopped, grasped what was taking place, and stared at the Buddha in amazement. Could it be that even the Buddha is straining to hear the words of the gospel? And if so, what wisdom had those giant ears, which can hear sounds both human and celestial, whether far or near, detected from the reading? Had he noticed too that I was no longer intimidated by his depth, that I was allowing myself to be Christian before him?

The temple stories end here. My first story was about the discovery that while Jesus is the central religious symbol in my world, he does not enter significantly into the world at large. People do find God without Jesus—this fact I already knew. What alarmed me was the awareness that a deep-seated uncertainty, hidden beneath my routine way of regarding Jesus, could break through so easily. The real Jesus was still somewhat of a stranger to me. The fact that one can be intimidated by the religious depths of another tradition shows, I think, how unreliable and untested routine faith is. I had arrived in Asia confident about Christianity—that Jesus was the truth of God. And I was discovering that my understanding of truth was limited. Jesus was probably not at all interested in making converts just so people would change their minds about the Buddha.

The second story is about hope. Yes, Jesus' words are meant for all nations to hear; but every Christian doctrine is not equally important. Yes, in Jesus one can encounter the divine presence; but one may have to let go of the Jesus of routine in order to find the Jesus who walks in unfamiliar places. I left Bodh-Gaya confident and happy: confident about my own religious heritage, joyful about the gospel's great possibilities for being listened to and welcomed in Asian hearts and minds. But I also went away with some freshly discovered questions about religious identity, about spiritual experience, and about the way God makes himself known within human history. They are the kinds of questions with which more and more Christians will have to wrestle, and so permit me to share how I have attempted to resolve them for myself.

Some people have wondered what being a Christian might be like in another two or three thousand years. How trustworthy will the Christian message sound to human beings whose faith would have to be threaded back to events which took place four or five millennia ago? The resurrection of Jesus will look like a tiny dot on the sands of time. What reasons will Christians of that age put forward in order to explain why they keep remembering the death of one man who lived such a long time ago? Perhaps human beings will eventually regard religion as having only antiquarian interest. Whatever churches and temples manage to survive would probably be maintained by a department of museums and parks. Undoubtedly, some intelligent people will have concluded that they can lead decent, peaceful lives without recourse to faith, while others will belong to a world religion—a religion more cosmic, more universal than any of the present world religions. That religion would amalgamate and teach the finest spiritual intuitions from every major system of belief. Only tradition-minded eccentrics would insist on interpreting their lives on the basis of events which took place in first-century Palestine.

Of course, the logic of historical distancing could pivot differently. Every major religion, it would be argued, has at least some stake in history; religious traditions, like wine, improve with age. No new religions of any consequence have arisen since the birth of Islam in the seventh century. A religion becomes more respectable the longer its beliefs have been seasoned by historical experience, the more its claims have been authenticated by the life-giving faith of people over many generations. A genuinely historical religion provides believers with a cultural and, in some cases, a transcultural identity. One expects to find Hindus in India and Buddhists in Thailand or Japan. But there are Muslims in countries as different as Indonesia and Iran, and Christianity has taken root in Africa, North and South America, as well as in the Philippines and other parts of the Far East. Religion spans national boundaries and historical periods; it often transcends ethnic differences by appealing to common human experience.

As a matter of fact, one might even venture the theological presumption that God would want to reveal himself early in human history—the earlier, the better—so as to show the path of salvation to as many people as possible. However, no religion would survive if it looked only to the past. Religions have to work now, in the present, or else people will abandon them. Major events of the past function as historical landmarks on the geography of faith; they help to identify the signs of God's presence in the history of a people. Those events may even become the nucleus of further religious experience. The people of Israel kept recalling the story of the Exodus: "Did not the Lord bring us up out of Egypt?" This constantly repeated reminder of God's faithfulness strengthened the faith of later generations, and Israel's story eventually enlightened Christians about the meaning of the deliverance which they experienced in Jesus. Christian baptism was sometimes viewed as a second exodus; future generations of Christians would keep recalling the way God had saved them in Jesus.

Whatever a religion remembers from the past has the power to interpret and shape the present and future. This is particularly true, I think, of Judaism and its cousin religions, Christianity and Islam. But Hinduism and Buddhism also have their stories to tell, even though their perspective on history centers less on particular events and attends more to the overall cycle of the entire human epic. In forgetting key elements of their stories, people risk losing their sense of direction within history and their reason for hope. God wants to meet people, and people have little chance of finding him apart from their religious tradition.

When people do not meet God, then something is amiss in the quality of their faith, their style of prayer, or the very doctrines of their religion. The light of mystery can grow dim because of human forgetfulness, moments of reverence become sparse, and doctrines can lose their power to disclose the religious experience of a tradition.

But the multiplicity of religions poses an added difficulty. Why would God initiate so many religions? Wouldn't the divine effort have appeared neater, more economical, if God had revealed just one religion for all? Besides, given the sorry fact that religions have frequently warred with one another, how can we be sure that God revealed himself through any of them? This leads into a second issue.

Each of the world religions would probably report a different experience of God. Each religion structures itself differently in terms of the language it uses to speak of God, the stories it tells, the doctrines it teaches, the particular symbols it ritualizes, the importance attached to sacred writings, and so on. Furthermore, no route to God bypasses a people's cultural expression. Because cultures differ, the way in which human beings experience time, the rhythms of life, the possibilities and limits of thinking and speaking about God, will also differ. Yet the fact that experiences of God are not the same does not set them automatically in opposition. There would be opposition, for instance, between a religious experience that promoted conquest and one that promoted freedom and forgiveness, or between a religious experience which ignored the neighbor and an experience that saw the neighbor as representing God. But I would argue further that conquest or neglect of one's neighbor cannot be the fruit of a genuine experience of God no matter what religion one belongs to.

The existence of many cultures demands, therefore, that God, in revealing himself to the human race at particular times and places, conform his grace to the variety of situations in which people live. As human beings try to express the contact with transcendence which they inwardly feel, they will naturally make use of the modes of religious expression—the words, ideas, stories, songs, and symbols—available to them through the culture in which they have grown up. If those religious forms prove too confining for the range and depth of one's inner experience, then one may have to borrow from another tradition, or else God will have to speak in a new key, in words and events that enable men and women to know what he is like.

The third issue that merits some comment is religious friction. There is an obvious difference between Christianity, Islamism, Hinduism, Buddhism, Taoism, and Judaism, on the one hand, and real live Christians, Muslims, Hindus, Buddhists, Taoists, and Jews, on the other hand. The reputation of a religion is often damaged by the behavior of its adherents; but the fact that believers commit sins does not discredit the religion to which they belong, at least in the case of the world's major religions.

Yet, what about comparing the various religions in terms of their beliefs? Surely, certain beliefs of one religion are incompatible with those of another religion; is that not so? Yes, I believe that some doctrines cannot be harmonized. The nature of the afterlife, views about divine justice, concepts of God, attitudes toward material creation: These often differ among individual religions. However, I am in no position to compare systems of belief. There is a still deeper question to be asked, a question that I am not able to answer either. Do all the religions lead to the same God?

Responding to this question requires a profound, intelligent, sympathetic encounter with the experience of another religious tradition. Some Christians have attempted this kind of meeting with another religion, which should hardly be surprising. Because Christians believe that the whole of creation and every genuine manifestation of God's presence take place through Christ, Christians are particularly eager for religious encounter in order to come to a richer understanding of the mystery of Christ. As Christians, we can recount how God has made himself known to us: He is the God and Father of our Lord Jesus Christ. But then we need to inquire of the Buddhist or the Muslim, "How has God made himself known to you?" There is no other way of finding out whether there is a holy oneness at the heart of the diverse religious traditions. And whenever believers, Christian or otherwise, feel defensive or threatened on account of another religion, they will be unable to learn; as long as they feel superior, they will be unable to teach. The Spirit's way of adding heart to religious dialogue may call for turning people poor, enabling them to cease clinging to their traditions and practices as if these things in themselves were the ground of religious identity and not the living God.

There is a famous legend in Buddhist folklore in which the Buddha compared preoccupation with settling the matter of God's existence to a man shot with a poisoned arrow. Before the victim would allow the arrow to be withdrawn and the wound treated, he insisted upon knowing who shot him, what sort of poison was killing him, what kind of medicine would be administered, and so on. Needless to say, the man died before his questions were answered. In the same way, the Buddha concluded, people need to be rescued from the burdens of suffering, craving, and ignorance, no matter how the issue of God's existence fares among the philosophers. I would have drawn a different conclusion: The wounded man could not be cured until he surrendered himself to the doctor, since no human being can be healed without trusting the one who shows the way to salvation. But on one point, we would agree: The time for salvation is now.

The arrow finds its target in each of us, although the moment of its striking differs from one life to another. "The Son of Man comes at an hour you least expect," says the gospel. But for each of us the time comes when we have to

31

ask about the goal and purpose of our living. Am I a person who responds to other people, and to the challenges of being fully human, in freedom, without hedging my bets or stalling on my commitment? Do I recognize the origin of my deepest desires for life and peace? Am I someone who is moved more by hope than by fear, one who trusts his or her capacity to love, one whose respect for the truth overcomes the temptation to take refuge in falsehood or compromise? The day on which such questions grab hold of us until we answer may be the hour when the Son of Man comes, that unexpected moment which calls for decision.

The reader might be wondering how I resolved the ambivalent feelings aroused by those episodes in the temples, for some resolution is necessary. Buddhists and Christians differ. Nothing is clarified by saying that Buddhism and Christianity are both religions, and that although their paths to salvation may be different, they aim for the same goal. That would be similar to comparing Marxists and capitalists, for example, and insisting that although they hold opposed views on political and economic issues, Marxists and capitalists share a common human nature; that they are thus essentially alike and only accidentally different. Or to use another example, the difference between believers and non-believers is not an accidental difference between two groups of people. The difference is basic. They define human nature in very different ways and they actualize two very different sets of human possibilities. I suspect that the same holds for Christians and Hindus, or Muslims and Buddhists. Becoming a person of God is the highest realization of human possibilities. To the degree that religions report differing experiences and understandings of God, they will also exhibit different models of realized holiness. To put the matter another way, Jesus is not the Buddha.

The Buddha taught his disciples not to rejoice when they were honored and praised, and to harbor no resentment when they were reviled and abused. They were to respect all forms of life, dwell in harmony with each other, and not to engage in fruitless speculation about the existence or nature of God. The Buddha also taught that the path to salvation or enlightenment required letting go of one's desire for personal survival after death.

These instructions should not sound unfamiliar to a Christian, not even the last lesson about renouncing one's ambitions for an afterlife. We look to God, not out of fear, nor out of the prospect of eternal rewards, but for God's own sake. Not our personal safety and survival, but the love and vision of God are alone worthy of our hope. Furthermore, the mysteries of the kingdom are not revealed to those who engage in clever speculation; the kingdom belongs to those who receive the gospel with the heart of a child.

As a matter of fact, the instructions which Jesus gives may not be so startlingly original when we reflect on them. By listening carefully to the words of the gospel, one often hears ideas that were somehow already known. Jesus' call to love, to forgive, to practice self-sacrifice and service, to grow in intimacy with a God who shows particular concern for the sinful and weak sounds neither strange nor impossible. The gospel puts us in touch with religious intuitions which have been unfolding deep within our subconscious groping for inner peace and grace. The New Testament reaffirms beliefs which we had already guessed to be well-founded: the superiority of grace over law, the power of the Spirit as liberating grace, the compassionate face of God, the courage that empowers us to believe that life, and not death, has the final claim upon us. It seems to me that we are able to hear what Jesus is saying in his parables and discourses, through his miracles and signs, because we also want to hear about our inner self. Or rather, Jesus explains us to ourselves. We want life and peace, and the gospel discloses the path of wisdom which leads to the fullness of life. But the disciples of the Buddha regarded the teaching of their master the same way.

33

Even the divinity of Christ may not be so exceptional as one might have thought. For Christian belief claims that all people have been created to share in God's nature. All of us, and not only Jesus, have been fashioned in God's image. The divinity of Christ, therefore, however special it is for Jesus' disciples, does not impose a heavy burden on our intelligence; the mind is ready to accept the possibility of men and women sharing in the very life of God. But then again, the Buddha also instructed his disciples about the way to enlightenment and Buddhahood; they were capable of achieving the same blessedness that their Lord had attained.

What about the Buddha's refusal to talk about God and his disdain for philosophical attempts to prove or disprove God's existence? Isn't this an abrogation of the mind's responsibility for ensuring that faith is well founded?

The Buddha was correct, I believe, when he protested that thinking about the existence or the non-existence of God ultimately profits nothing. Indeed, there is an appropriate time and place in the course of our lives for coming to terms intellectually with the issue of God's existence and determining exactly what we believe. Some features of the world and of our experience point toward God, some areas are either silent or inconclusive about God, and other aspects of life argue against God's existence or his care for the world. But the thinking stage cannot last forever. We arrive at a point where further thinking solves nothing. The sun will continue to rise and set, the business of daily living proceeds, many important questions will remain unanswered, but we still experience ourselves as inwardly unfree, not at peace with our deeper self, insecure about our hold on life and our reasons for hope. Some men and women pass to a stage in their lives where they keep on believing in God without intellectually resolving the issue of God's existence. But what could this possibly mean?

If too much time is spent on weighing the pros and cons of faith, the mind will sooner or later become so exhausted that the question of God's existence ceases to be critical; it may even cease to be intelligible. A prolonged hesitation about committing oneself to the consequences of believing in God will make the soul's energies shrivel like the skin of a prune. The soul's great power for hope will remain un-engaged. Though it may sound paradoxical, I think it can be said that the religious dimension of human existence appears strongest in people so saturated with faith that they cannot conceive the world with God or without God. They can no longer determine what difference the existence of God would make to their way of viewing the world. Why? Because for them God pervades life so completely that they do not know how to point to him. Their perception of God's presence is no longer directed to one particular time or place.

"You Christians find God in reality," someone once remarked, "but I find reality without God." To anyone who has sunk deep roots into the soil of faith, this comment will probably sound hollow. Indeed, there are many people whose living has been tempered by events which pulled from their souls the prayer, "Lord, I do believe; help me overcome my unbelief!" They find it difficult to describe God. They do not understand him as a person in the usual sense of the word, and even in calling God "Father" they realize that God transcends gender. They do not understand God to be some thing which can be either discovered or missed in reality, depending upon one's point of view. If that were the case, then one would not be talking about God but about a celestial light fixture, an imaginary guardian of human affairs. Once the meaning of the word "God" is com-prehended, the matter of God's existence seems to take care of itself.

Some spiritual writers, especially those from the Eastern Christian tradition, teach that God appears as darkness to us. Once in that darkness, we are in God. But God does not dwell in darkness. He is not secretive, nor is he a cosmic riddle which our minds are simply unable to fathom. And yet, in moving closer to God, the mind stalls in what can be described as a dark cloud, like the cloud that enveloped Moses when he climbed up to Mount Sinai. However, the soul's inner experience stays sharply directed. The heart drifts toward forgiving, trusting, loving, even to taking up the cross, as if such activity were the soul's natural motions. For some spiritual writers, the cross of Jesus symbolizes divine abandonment, Jesus' experience of a God who receded into darkness. "From the sixth hour until the ninth hour," Matthew wrote in his gospel, "darkness came over all the land." But there was nothing dark about the motions of Jesus' soul. He could still forgive his enemies, he was gracious to a repentant thief, he was concerned about his mother's welfare, and he entrusted himself to his Father's hands.

Perhaps, then, the cross reveals something more than the experience of divine abandonment, for abandonment may be simply the first wave of feeling which overtakes us when we approach the darkness of God. Perhaps the cross is also telling us how much God and darkness are inseparable. When words and images for describing God lose their punch, when our past experiences of God seem to fall apart as we try to reconstruct them, when the mind is no longer sure whether God exists in any form in which we had so far recognized him, when the question of his existence or non-existence loses its relevance, then perhaps one is entering the silent stillness of God. Eyes close, ears stretch, hands open, and one learns to see inwardly, to listen carefully, to receive gratefully, and to wait patiently for the coming of wisdom.

The Buddha realized that all human beings must submit to the conditions of creaturehood. All of us are limited and finite, and all must die. But every religion does not thematize the experience of creaturehood the same way. The Buddha had emphasized the fleeting nature of earthly beauty; he taught his disciples to look beneath the surface of material things and to be aware of the corruption and decay undermining everything. Christians would be acquainted with the same idea from the Book of Ecclesiastes in the Old Testament. In my notebook, I had copied a portion of one of the Buddha's discourses:

> "And what, monks, is the satisfaction in material shapes? Monks, it is like a girl in a noble's family or a brahman's family or a householder's family who at the age of fifteen or sixteen is not too tall, not too short, not too thin, not too fat, not too dark, not too fair—is she, monks, at the height of her beauty and loveliness at that time?"

> "Yes, Lord."

> "Monks, whatever happiness and pleasure arise because of beauty and loveliness, this is satisfaction in material shapes. And what, monks, is peril in material shapes? As to this, monks, one might see that same lady after a time, eighty or ninety or a hundred years old, aged, crooked as a rafter, bent, leaning on a stick, going along palsied, miserable, youth gone, teeth broken, hair thinned, skin wrinkled, stumbling along, the limbs discolored. What would you think, monks? That which was former beauty and loveliness has vanished, a peril has appeared?"

> "Yes, Lord."

> "This too, monks, is a peril in material shapes. And again, monks, one might see that same lady diseased, suffering, sorely ill, lying in her own excrement, having to be lifted up by others, having to be laid down by others. What would you think, monks? That that which was former beauty and loveliness has vanished, a peril has appeared?"

> "Yes, Lord."

This line of thinking is pursued to the decomposing of the

woman's corpse, its being devoured by crows and jackals, and its bones being reduced to powder.

Such a discourse would make salutary Ash Wednesday reading. Some Christian writers have made the grimness of mortality the centerpiece of their faith. But death and finiteness did not trouble Jesus. The created universe, even with its laws of death and decay, can be tender with moments of beauty and hope. The world has more to say about itself, I think, than the Buddha heard. The Hindu poet, Rabindranath Tagore, put it this way:

> Deliverance is not for me in renunciation. I feel the embrace of freedom in a thousand bonds of delight.
>
> Thou ever pourest for me the fresh draught of thy wine of various colors and fragrance, filling this earthen vessel to the brim.
>
> My world will light its hundred different lamps with thy flame and place them before the altar of thy temple.
>
> No, I will never shut the doors of my senses. The delights of sight and hearing and touch will bear thy delight.

The Christian would make a different case too. Because of our belief that in Jesus the Word of God took flesh and joined the human story, the Christian's attitude toward materiality cannot be the same as the Buddhist's. The resurrection of Jesus reverses our perception of death and decay. Without denying mortality, we dare to hope that the universe will not disappoint those who want to see the face of God.

The Buddha's warning that the speculations of theologians and philosophers about the nature of God will not bring salvation to anyone is well founded. I had engaged in a great deal of thinking and speculating myself; but speculation is not the same thing as faith. No human being can grow and develop without faith. All have to learn how to trust—how to trust another's promises and how to accept another's love. Call it human faith, but without the ability to believe and trust others, a person will not become fully human.

In the same way, we need to learn how to trust the universe, to believe that the earth is meant to be the home of the human family, and to have faith that human life is indeed a gracious gift. No one understands the mystery of God who has not learned how to respond to life with trusting surrender. No other response does full justice to both the needs and the possibilities of the human soul.

The difference between Jesus and the Buddha shows itself in one other way. Instead of withdrawing from the world after he had received enlightenment beneath the bo tree, the Buddha remained with his monks in order to instruct them about the path to salvation. But that path led to transcending the world. Two different religious worlds are represented in the Buddha seated in life-transcending contemplation and Jesus nailed to life through the wood of the cross. These two symbols say a great deal about religious experience and about the attitudes of Buddhists and Christians toward creation.

From a Christian perspective, the possibility of religious experience depends on the fact that men and women can be attracted and drawn to something outside themselves. The created universe is not to be ignored but noticed; we study it, paint it, write stories and songs about it, and find pleasure or sadness in its contrasting moods. As St. Thomas reasoned, human beings are naturally contemplative because their ultimate destiny is to be caught up in the vision of God. Any process of meditation which does not draw people out of themselves turns into mind-controlling technique.

Now I am not proposing that people should be reluctant to develop their inner space and mental powers. But what catches our attention has to be something besides our own self with its preoccupations and its tendency to revel in self-centered dreaming. One of the worst possible nightmares is dreaming that we have died and fallen into an absolute, isolated silence where no one would ever hear or touch us again. And one of the most relaxing dreams would find us in the company of those whom we love, surprised at how many people had cared for us even though we were unaware of it during our lifetime, and happy because every pain of separation had been overcome.

Dreams like these indicate how we have been made. I doubt that human beings could ever arrive at a lasting inner peace without being drawn into the lives of others; they must care for one another, pray for others, weep with others, laugh with others, and even sometimes die with others. Jesus made this clear. And that is why the contemplative silence of Christian experience moves to the heart of the world: to suffer with it, to hope with it, to repent with it, and to rise with it. Is this what the Buddha strained to hear? I hope it was.

This brief apology for Christian faith cannot be extended to include everything about Christianity. It is important to understand that Christianity, as it is often explained and presented, may not necessarily be the purest form of religiousness available to the human spirit. Even with its devotions, its cult of the saints, its sacraments and liturgical forms, its sacred books and doctrines, Christianity is not automatically the contemplation and simple adoration of God. And this is why we must be ready to turn poor. No matter how consoling or spiritually gratifying religious practices may be in themselves, religion must wind up in God. No one can be forced to believe in God, and no one can control the divine presence. Unless we are ready to accept that many men and women have found God even though they never encountered Jesus, that many religious people have had their sins forgiven even though they never heard of the Christian sacrament of reconciliation, and that many Christians have come close to God although they did not receive the Eucharist regularly, then we are probably not prepared to accept God as God truly is, with all the splendor and incomprehensible contours of his grace.

For us who have grown so accustomed to viewing our religion in terms of the "fullness of truth" and blessed with the riches of scripture and sacrament, turning poor so as to hear how God has blessed people within other religious traditions presents a hard challenge. Only God can fill the emptiness within the human soul; without faith, religious observances will not bring us near to God. But grace and the means of grace, God and the various expressions of institutional religion, ought not to be confused. Otherwise we run the risk of concluding, for example, that by defending sacramental practice, papal infallibility, the inerrancy of the Bible, or the existence of hell, we are coming to the rescue of God himself. Believing Jesus to be the Son of God and Second Person of the Trinity, one must beware of taking another step and attaching divine approval to nearly every aspect of Christian religion. We have to avoid appealing too often and too confidently, even in the privacy of our own thoughts, to the way we believe things really are. Such appeals generally boil down to the claim that God is on our side and therefore that every other church or religion is mistaken, provisional, or inadequate. A religion may indeed posture itself this way, but no religion can manipulate or command the divine presence.

I don't mean to concede too much, either. I want merely to say that one has to become poor in order to know God and that this disposition toward poverty regulates the inner spirit of our religion. The point may be clearer once I have explained what poverty might mean for us who are materially advantaged. This will be the subject of the next two chapters. In this chapter I have been drawing out some long thoughts about religion that were provoked by the unsteadying effect of being a Christian in unfamiliar religious places. One starts to learn that even our thinking about God needs to turn poor. Yes, questions about God and the world religions will arise and call for resolution. Yes, Christian thinkers and monks, Christian pilgrims and Christian mystics will help the rest of us to pick our way through the strange territory of religious diversity. Yet thoughts about God will not be enough to purchase salvation. Thoughts about God pass through his mystery like ships sliding over the ocean; thoughts about God leave us unchanged. Instead, God has to pass through our minds, taking out the knots which have snarled our inner vision. As God passes through us, he enables our minds to pass unobstructed through the needle's eye.

# Interlude 1

Times of transition can be hard to live through, but the passing is made easier if we believe that there is some direction or purpose unfolding in our lives. We can bear the tension of growth, the inconvenience and confusion of change, if we discern that the Spirit has been urging, needling, and inspiring us forward. This holds true for us as individuals; it also holds true for us as a church.

The early church's transition from the world of Palestine to the wider world of the Roman Empire did not occur without a little suffering and a lot of foot-dragging. As Luke tells us in the Acts of the Apostles, there were those who hoped for a speedy return of Jesus to Jerusalem, to tie up the loose ends of his redemptive work, to judge sinners and reward the faithful, and then to lead his followers into glory. There were others who resented the church's gradual departure from Jewish ways. As far as the Spirit was concerned, the church would have to learn how to turn religiously poor. This meant that some Christians had to let go of their wish for Jesus' immediate return, and other Christians had to let go of a few cherished religious traditions. But the Spirit of Jesus was with them and ahead of them. Once they recognized the way the Spirit was moving in their lives and in their moment of history, as St. Luke did, then the transition became a moment of grace.

There is reason to think that we are experiencing a similar transition today, although our perception of the Spirit's action has yet to be clarified. We need men and women like St. Luke to help us discern the Spirit's direction and purpose in the events of our time. The encounter of the world religions is something new, and the possibilities which await us might appear sometimes disturbing, sometimes breathtaking. But the Spirit will not move us without first turning us poor, that is, without our letting go of some habitual ways of thinking about the church and religion. And if the Spirit is stirring the religious waters, then we have no reason to be disheartened by what we see or hear: People are discovering what it means to be religious.

Centering one's attention on God is not always easy. How can we not be distracted by all the things we are doing each day, the chores which have yet to be finished, the material things which we want to own, the daily routine which keeps us from being imaginative or from noticing something new? I am not suggesting that we should cease from all our business and give away everything we possess. But centering on God is made difficult when we don't know what we should be looking at. There is no way to find God, and so to find the truth about ourselves and our historical moment, without turning inwardly poor. For the fact is, I think, that human beings are already poor, but this is a fact which many people fail to understand. Ultimately, all of us are powerless—or poor—it makes little difference here. Realizing this fact means passing through a number of elementary and often painful human experiences. Centering on God, then, requires being poor. "Blessed are the poor in spirit," Matthew might have said, "for they will see God." Blessed are those whom the Spirit makes poor, for they will find the God who makes all things new.

# 2

## Poverty and Truth

They love truth when it enlightens them, they hate
truth when it accuses them. Because they do not wish
to be deceived and do wish to deceive, they love truth
when it reveals itself, and hate it when it reveals them.
Thus it shall reward them as they deserve: Those who
do not wish to be revealed by truth, truth will unmask
against their will, but it will not reveal itself to them.

Saint Augustine

The beggar children asleep under the railway bridge are
poor. The man with the facial cancer in Mother Teresa's
House for the Dying in Calcutta is poor. The mother with
the three thin children waiting for her ration of rice is poor.
The wealthy parents whose daughter went insane
discovered that they are poor. They lost a child, and though
they had plenty of money, they were unable to buy what
they wanted most. The clergyman at a loss for sympathetic
and consoling words is also poor; his is the poverty of an
empty heart.

Among the ranks of the world's poor, the physically
poor are understandably included. But shouldn't we also list
the culturally deprived—people imprisoned in a flat
universe, unrelieved by great ideas, music, literature, and
art? Why not also the spiritually poor—those confined to a
world that never shows itself to be a gift, people who have
no knowledge of God? We could also add the affectively
poor, men and women who starve for want of love and ac-
ceptance; and the morally poor, people unable to break the
vicious circle of compromise, disgrace, and self-contempt.
The insides of the spiritually, culturally, or affectively im-

45

poverished look like what the homeless and hungry are out-side.

There is no doubt that material poverty and the lack of education are linked, and where knowledge provides the only access to the hallways of power and prestige, the poor will be permanently locked out. But where knowledge primarily means wisdom and not power, the poor may stand an easier chance of finding it. The question we have to ask is, Who are the poor? Material deprivation can drive people to greed and revolution as easily as it can draw them to wisdom, while material security often turns people into oppressors as they figure out ways of maintaining their privileges and steer away from some of life's elementary lessons about being human. However, learning and finan-cial security can also assure people enough self-esteem and independence from basic material needs to think about their neighbors and to care for them.

Throughout the Bible, the chorus of the poor com-plains to God and cries for justice. The poor have no other recourse. Theirs is a prayer that most of us will never have to make, except allegorically. This also means that most of us will never have the satisfaction of knowing how reliable our faith is: Does our faith really rest in God, or is our faith assisted by the political system, the financial institutions, the technological know-how, and industrial capacity which actually insure our well-being and security from day to day? If the story of Job can be taken as an example, the tale of the upright and prosperous man who was thrown into physical and financial ruin, then we have cause to wonder whether God is likely to allow faith to go unexercised. Sooner or later, we may find ourselves in a chorus we would not will-ingly have joined.

In this chapter, I want to explore the relationship be-tween truth and poverty, for they are related. Their rela-tionship is composed of two interior events. First, truth often strikes people when they have become spiritually poor, that is, when they have tasted what it is like to be powerless. Second, the experience of being poor is itself one of truth's bald moments, whether one recognizes it or not. But the *power of truth* can be experienced and recognized. Deprived of the trappings of success, people are primed to feel the hand of God as clay awaits the touch of the potter. And so Gerard Manley Hopkins wrote: "Over again I feel thy finger and find thee." I think this line could serve as a beautiful gloss on a famous text from Jeremiah:

> So I went down to the potter's house, and I saw him working at the wheel. But the pot he was shaping from the clay was marred in his hands; so the potter formed it into another pot, shaping it as seemed best to him (Jer 18:3 4).

Who then are the poor? They are, first of all, those who carry the burden of human injustice: the destitute, those without land or property or political voice, those with none to comfort them in their grief. But this kind of poverty need not, in and of itself, crack the human soul open to realizing its radical dependence on God. Whenever scripture depicts God and his prophets championing the side of the poor, it does so under the presumption that God alone has become their hope and refuge. Without God, poverty can turn the human soul into stone. And so there is a poverty which the human soul experiences as it awakens to the fact that everything in the world belongs to God; this is the ultimate truth about us. No one learns this truth without first turning poor.

## A Clarification About Truth

Although truth is often referred to in the plural—as if there were many truths—it seems to me that basically there is only one truth, and that truth is God. Human beings become truthful only to the degree that they are people of God, people in whom God lives.

Coming to the truth involves quite a bit more than discovering the reasonableness of a position or establishing the correctness of an idea. That is why people can fail to reach agreement about the truth even though there is nothing logically faulty in their process of reasoning and even though they accept the same facts. Truth is a different matter than correctness because truth cannot be apprehended apart from faith. Truth is what makes the human spirit live and breathe. Only those ideas which are capable of growing in us, or rather which cause us to grow, deserve to be called truths. The gospel becomes a truth and ceases to be only a narrative of the life and teaching of Jesus when the words and actions of Jesus begin to breathe with us and to transform our minds and wills. An accurate indicator of truth is the power which certain beliefs have to transform men and women into people who are more open, more inwardly free, more capable of selfless love, ready to trust, and who are at peace with themselves. Nevertheless, the fact that we often speak of truth in the plural should not distract us from seeing that truth is essentially one: Whatever we call truth, whatever ideas or beliefs are spoken of as truths, should draw us to the one truth which is God. And poverty disposes the human spirit to hear and respond to the voice of truth.

### Poverty and Gratitude

In his work *The Dark Night of the Soul*, St. John of the Cross drew attention to the connection between poverty and truth when he wrote that during the "dark contemplation" the soul experiences "an emptiness and poverty" with respect to temporal, natural, and spiritual goods. The soul feels "terrible annihilation in its very substance and extreme poverty"; it tastes "its own intimate poverty and misery." As a result of this contemplation, however, a person becomes meek toward God and himself, and also toward his neighbor. As a result he will no longer become impatiently angry with himself and his faults, nor with his neighbor's, neither is he displeased or disrespectfully querulous with God for not making him perfect quickly.

The purgation of the dark night leaves the soul stripped of every attachment, cleansed of every material, psychological, and spiritual crutch through which it formerly found security. What remains is the soul's naked desire for the God who lies at the soul's center, hidden in its veins.

When the soul enters its dark night, its purgatory on earth, it starts to feel that inner poverty which is not so readily recognized in its day-to-day routine. The soul becomes aware that it can never be a real owner, for however rich or talented we may be, we actually own nothing. We possess nothing. We are incapable of *having* anything. No material object, no person or relationship, no memory, no skill, no savings account, can be protected from the steady encroachment of time. Time may be ours to spend, but time is not ours to own. Objects perish, people die, relationships fade unless regularly attended to, skills laboriously developed grow stale, treasured ideas pass out of season.

"Don't swear by the heavens," Jesus warned, because God owns them. "Or by the earth," because the earth belongs to God too. "Or by your own head," for we do not even belong to ourselves. At the bottom line about human existence, it is clear that we do not even *have* life, since no power on earth can entitle us to live here forever. Our hold on health, on faith, and on our future, is awfully slender. Least of all can we lay claim to God. Finally, the soul realizes in its dark night, it is God who has us. T. S. Eliot wrote in the *Four Quartets*:

For most of us, there is only the unattended
Moment, the moment in and out of time,
The distraction fit, lost in a shaft of sunlight,
The wild thyme unseen, or the winter lightning
Or the waterfall, or music heard so deeply
That it is not heard at all, but you are the music
While the music lasts.

Poverty describes the basic truth about the human condition; to be human is to be poor. John of the Cross detailed the painful ascent by which human beings arrive at this truth, and he called this knowledge humility. The soul's dark night burns away from our minds and hearts every illusion about real ownership and possession. Without an experience of the soul's profound emptiness, it is not possible to encounter the living God. Poverty is like the soul's Advent season, its mood of patient but intense longing for the Lord's coming; poverty is the alarm that calls us to "attend to the moment."

Oddly enough, genuine gratitude to God emerges from the soul's engagement with its inner poverty. In her autobiography, St. Teresa of Avila tells of her struggle to develop an honest gratitude to God. Why the struggle? The problem which Teresa uncovered centered, I think, on the difference between human giving and divine giving. In human relationships, people *exchange* gifts. There is a mutual giving of gifts—whether immediately, as at Christmas, or throughout the course of a year, as at birthdays and anniversaries. Etiquette and custom have conditioned us to think that if someone brings us a gift (especially if the gift comes as a total surprise, for no special occasion), or if someone invites us to dinner, then at a later date we ought to return the kindness. The thoughtful friend who put us in a debt which could not be repaid would upset the social balance between us.

Now what about our relationship with God? What return can we make to God for all that he has given to us?

The fact is that we do not owe God anything, since God never gives a gift in order to place us in his debt. His giving is pure; he gives simply because he is good. Our inability to repay God, the misguided belief that God needs or expects to be repaid, and the awkwardness of wondering how to respond to kindness which is so entirely undeserved, leaves the soul uncomfortable and confused. Our relationship with God cannot be squared away, like a social obligation waiting to be satisfied. Indeed, there is nothing we have which has not been given to us, as Teresa knew. By thinking that we could repay God for some of his kindness, however well intentioned the sentiment, we merely pretend to ourselves that we are not poor. This is the lesson that Teresa discovered. After all, how could we live, how would we draw the next moment's breath, how could our minds be illumined in a moment of inspiration, unless God granted it? Those who are acquainted with their poverty also understand themselves; they are set free to be genuinely grateful.

A relationship to God will not mature to the degree that it is planted in feelings of guilt or inadequacy over our failures to thank God enough, or as long as we feel unsure about whether God has been pleased by our modest attempts at repayment. In realizing that one does not have the means to make even the smallest return for the least of God's favors, one starts to notice the giver rather than the gifts and to celebrate God's loving kindness. In fact, Jesus told a parable about this:

> Then Jesus said to his host, "When you give a luncheon or a dinner, do not invite your friends, your brothers or relatives, or your rich neighbors; if you do, they may invite you back and so you will be repaid. But when you give a banquet, invite the poor, the crippled, the lame, the blind, and you will be blessed. Although they cannot repay you, you will be repaid at the resurrection of the righteous" (Lk 14:12-14).

51

"Invite those who cannot repay": But this is exactly what God has done! God enjoys the satisfaction of giving solely because of love. Perhaps the repayment which Jesus promised will be nothing less than the opportunity to participate in the divine experience of giving.

The language which 16th-century writers like Teresa of Avila and John of the Cross used to describe their inner experience may be culturally distant from us. Dark nights, spiritual senses, and mystical marriages do not form part of our ordinary religious vocabulary, although the experiences behind these expressions seem to ride across the centuries. In order to understand the process of turning inwardly poor, each of us today could probably identify a set of experiences where we have wrestled with the strange grace that draws us to see our real poverty.

## The Strange Grace of Turning Poor

In his novel, *A Death in the Family*, James Agee recalled the memory of a child's chilling experience of waking in the middle of the night, frightened by the "huge, ragged mouth" of darkness. Agee wrote:

Darkness said:

When is this meeting, child, where are we, who are you, child, who are you, do you know who you are, do you know who you are, child; are you?

He knew that he would never know, though memory, almost captured, unrecapturable, unbearably tormented him. That this little boy whom he inhabited was only the cruellest of deceits. That he was but the nothingness of nothingness, condemned by some betrayal, condemned to be aware of nothingness. That yet in that desolation, he was not without companions. For featureless on the abyss, invincible, moved monstrous intuitions. And from the depth and wide throat of eternity burned the cold, delirious chuckle of rare monsters, cruelty beyond cruelty.

Who has not occasionally awakened in the middle of the night, startled by the silent emptiness of a dark room and terrified by the prospect that one night will have to be the last night of one's life? Faces parade before the mind's eye—some belonging to people already dead, some which have not been seen for a long time, still others belonging to people very dear and close. Who has not shivered at the thought that people who are now so important and loved must also pay their dues to that yawning darkness? No horror movie ever promised an ending so sure and dreadful. Death is fearsome, and it seems to set loose its worst assaults in the middle of the night.

To calm our fear, we might turn on a lamp or radio, walk around the room and recall the number of hours until daylight. We might want to pray, but frequently our aloneness, sharpened by fear, shatters the prayer into syllables, the syllables into letters, and the letters into particles which vanish in the air. "I cried out to God for help," said the Psalmist, "I cried out to God to hear me." Had the Psalmist too been startled from sleep?

> When I was in distress, I sought
>     the Lord;
> at night I stretched out untiring
>     hands
> and my soul refused to be
>     comforted.
>
> I remembered you, O God, and I
>     groaned;
> I mused, and my spirit grew faint (Ps 77:2-3).

Have you ever stood by the sea and let your thoughts be sprayed clean by the crashing of the waves? Have you sat on the brow of a hill and watched how the clouds make shadows across a valley? Have you ever held a child in your lap and made silly faces until it laughed, or opened the door to a surprise visit from someone you love? Have you fingered wheat as it was sprouting, explored a trail through the woods, or cheered the performance of a symphony? Have you cried over disappointment, or waited anxiously for the safe return of a husband or wife, a son or daughter, a brother or sister, or your closest friend? Have you been moved to prayer by the sufferings of people you never met?

There are thousands of experiences, moments, and concerns like these which give texture, shape, and color to life. Even our tears reveal just how much we care for the earth and all the things which happen here. How then shall we take leave of this world—a world of such beauty, of warm memories and dear friends—without saying a word of thanks to whomever or whatever has been responsible for the sheer grace of our being here? But are human beings meant to behold the face of God? Or in addition to surrendering life, must we also give up our minds to everlasting darkness?

And who might this Lord be whose traces appear everywhere yet whose presence is so easily doubted? Who has ever seen or touched him? Does God have a clearly discernible voice? Even as words of gratitude begin taking form on our lips, the mind sometimes starts to wonder whether anyone was ever "there" in the first place. When a human being finally flowers into a person who is deeply thankful, clean-souled, and open-hearted to the point of being vulnerable to compassion, does any divine eye perceive this great achievement of human spirit? Or do moments of intense spiritual growth evaporate unnoticed into the vast cosmic night? That prayer which issues from the heart so earnestly and thankfully in the morning can turn dull and tasteless by nightfall. The 20th-century theologian, Henri de Lubac, wrote in *The Discovery of God*:

> Why is it that the mind which has found God still retains or constantly reverts to, the feeling of not having

found him? Why does the absence weigh on us even in
the presence itself, however intimate it may be? Why,
face to face with him who penetrates all things, why
that insurmountable obstacle, that unbridgeable gap?
Why always a wall or a gaping void? Why do all
things, as soon as they have shown him to us, betray
us by concealing him again?

To some people, this line of reflection will appear to
lack faith; it will suggest uncertainty and fear where religion
should be demonstrating conviction and power.

I believe, however, that questions like these signify
how terribly poor the human spirit is. There is so much
about ourselves, about where we came from and where we
are heading, about our deepest motives, about the purity
and sincerity of our prayer, that escapes our comprehension. And yet, the desire to conquer our fears honestly, to
develop a liberating confidence in the intelligibility of the
universe, to set our hearts on what is life-giving, also
belongs to the truth about us. We have hope, and it is that
hope which empowers us to keep thinking and praying over
what the earth and our experiences are telling us about
ourselves.

Morning reprieves us from the terror and loneliness of
the night. Personal doubts and private fears look like
harmless shadows once the sun's light begins pouring over
the earth. But the taste of poverty will linger in our
memories to remind us at a later time who and what we are.
Those who have tasted poverty understand why so many
voices from the Bible speak of trusting and hoping in God.
"You will not fear the terror of night," said the Psalmist,
"nor the pestilence that stalks the darkness." Poor people
place their trust in God because, finally, there is nothing
else.

Truth happens to us, so to speak, when we live out that
native poverty which marks every man and woman as

someone created from the clay of the earth and the kiss of God's breath. Poverty pulls away the mask of prestige, of knowledge, of social class, or of strength—whatever it is that we use to command attention and respect. Poverty enables us to hear the gospel's truth, the words of life which God addresses to the world in Christ. Truth is powerful. The gospel manages to break through human pretense and warns us of the penalties which will come from refusing to hear the word of life. From individuals, societies, nations, and whole civilizations, the truth exacts a high price for failing to listen to the words which have been spoken for their peace.

### God and the Prophet: A Lesson in Turning Poor

The prophets of the Old Testament help to illustrate the connection between knowing the Lord and becoming poor. They were people who could not live with the Lord's word without suffering the poverty of their own spirit. They endured the range of a poor person's experience. They were often physically powerless before their enemies, they had to wait patiently for and then boldly announce a word which did not belong to them, their faith was strained by the slowness of God's justice, and they frequently found themselves alone and rejected because of their zeal for the word of the Lord. Given a list of the world's least desirable occupations, I suspect that the Old Testament prophet would be ranked at the top.

St. Paul welcomed prophecy as a great gift to the church, because the prophet's appearance within a community indicated that the Spirit was active in its midst. However, the prophets of Israel did not always receive enthusiastic welcomes. The Letter of James reads: "Brothers, as an example of patience in the face of suffering, take the prophets who spoke in the name of the Lord" (Jas 5:10). And speaking of prophets and other champions of faith, the Letter to the Hebrews tells us:

Some faced jeers and flogging, while still others were chained and put in prison. They were stoned; they were sawed in two; they were put to death by the sword. They went about in sheepskins and goatskins, destitute, persecuted, and mistreated—the world was not worthy of them. They wandered in deserts and mountains, and in caves and holes in the ground (Heb 11:36-38).

Jesus was well aware of the life expectancy of a prophet, as Matthew records:

"Therefore, I am sending you prophets and wise men and teachers. Some of them you will kill and crucify; others you will flog in your synagogues and pursue from town to town. And so upon you will come all the righteous blood that has been shed on earth, from the blood of righteous Abel to the blood of Zechariah, son of Berakiah, whom you murdered between the temple and the altar" (Mt 23:34-35).

Jeremiah was dropped into the muddy bottom of a cistern, John the Baptist was beheaded in Herod's dungeon, Elijah had walked through the wilderness 40 days and nights to reach Horeb, the mountain of God; and to make matters worse, once he reached the mountain God asked him, "What are you doing here, Elijah?" (1 Kgs 19:13). As if God didn't know!

Clearly, the human capacity to resist the word of truth assumes ugly proportions, even into our own day.

The prophet's cool reception is somewhat understandable. After all, his message could slice through the behavior and nerves of his listeners. Amos called the faithless women of Israel "cows of Bashan" who would be dragged away with fish hooks (Amos 4:1ff). Jeremiah compared the king of Judah and his court to a bunch of rotten figs and forecast 70 years of exile (Jer 24-25). John the Baptist called the crowds who assembled to hear him a "brood of vipers" (Lk

3:7), and Jesus told the Pharisees and teachers of the Law that they were whitewashed tombs (Mt 23:27). Who would dare to embark on so perilous a career unless God had personally summoned him to be a prophet and burned his words on the prophet's lips?

The moment of truth is unpredictable. The prophet's calling has never been regulated because the Spirit's power cannot be brought under the thumb of any human institution. Neither church nor temple could determine who would be a prophet; that choice fell to the Spirit of God. To be sure, in the New Testament period the spiritual gift of discernment enabled the community to identify authentic prophets. Unfortunately, the church gradually institutionalized its function of discerning and, in the process, managed to push the prophets from both pulpit and pew.

The prophets of Israel did not gaze into crystal balls, either. You don't have to be a wizard to know, for example, that your nation's future lies in jeopardy when many of your fellow citizens are concerned only with amassing wealth, when they show no sympathy for the defenseless poor, or when your political leaders create military ties with godless men. The prophet was convinced that the words he spoke to the people had been given to him by God. It was not the word of Isaiah, nor the word of Jeremiah, nor the word of Ezekiel, but the word of the Lord which had to be delivered. In the gospel of John we are told that even Jesus spoke only those words he had received from his Father:

> The words I say to you are not just my own. Rather, it is the Father, living in me, who is doing his work (Jn 14:10).

> For I gave them the words you gave me and they accepted them (17:8).

> I do nothing on my own but speak just what the Father has taught me (8:28).

Isaiah had his lips purged of every impurity with burning coals, Ezekiel ate the scroll which God handed him, Jeremiah's mouth was touched by the finger of God, and the Spirit itself descended upon Jesus at his baptism in the Jordan. The word of God came to them freely and graciously. They did not own it, they could not determine the time and place of its coming, and they could not avoid the mission it imposed. The coming of God's word was not a magical infusion of otherworldly wisdom and it could not be forced upon the people by the prophet's will. The coming of God's word was a moment of truth and grace in which the prophet's vision of the world was clarified by the Spirit.

Where are the Jeremiahs, the Daniels and Joels, the Elijahs and Hoseas of today? Or are the prophets a lost breed, people of whom the world is unworthy, as the Letter to the Hebrews put it?

The real problem is not the whereabouts of the prophets—they are very much with us. The basic issue concerns the world's receptivity to God's word. The prophetic voice purifies and cleanses, even as the prophet's lips are burned clean by the fire of divine feeling. The prophetic word may console the oppressed but it stings the powerful. The prophet's message makes us face up to our native poverty and dependence upon God, it turns us defenseless and poor by uncovering the hollowness of untested faith. Who would give glad welcome to this kind of word?

Nevertheless, God's word still comes. The moment of truth which a prophetic word or action invites is always a grace, even though it grates on the world's religious, political, or social nerves. That word is a sign of the Spirit's activity in our midst. It cannot be forced upon people by one who does not have it, and neither state nor church has the power to arrest it. Because God does indeed care for the world, his word will continue to confront us with a clarified vision of life, challenging us to change our loyalties and to deepen our understanding of what really matters.

Witnesses to the gospel's truth live and move among us: teachers, preachers, men and women of conviction and faith whose words and example unleash storms in the world's soul. Christians and non-Christians alike, they are the people who have been imprisoned or exiled for refusing to serve in war, put on trial for protesting the spread of nuclear arms, ridiculed for demonstrating against abortion clinics, ambushed by police in Central America, consigned to mental hospitals in the Soviet Union, labeled Marxists and Communists for quoting from the gospels and writings of the popes, or murdered at the altar. Such people dramatize the cleaving edge of God's truth and the violence aroused by the teaching of Jesus. "Do you think I came to bring peace on the earth? No, I tell you, but division" (Lk 12:51).

Conversion means turning poor, and it means violence. No one is born into the kingdom of God apart from that violence which is sin's resistance to grace.

I do not want to spell out here how individuals or communities should proceed in authenticating a prophetic voice. The critical issue here concerns the dynamics set loose inside of us when someone's words or actions become a prophetic challenge. We find ourselves startled, resisting, examining, praying, summoning up the courage to respond. Or we may reject the message because we don't like the tone of the prophet's voice, or are dismayed by the prophet's tactics, or don't approve of the prophet's dress and departure from religious style, or are repelled by the boldness of the one who confronts respectable people. But decision cannot be avoided, and once we start checking the prophet's credentials, the time for deciding may have passed. We shall already have made our response to the truth and then have fallen into quibbling over the prophet's background and competence. This is exactly what the townsfolk of Nazareth did:

Coming to his home town, he began teaching the people in their synagogue, and they were amazed. "Where did this man get this wisdom and these miraculous powers?" they asked. "Isn't this the carpenter's son? Isn't his mother's name Mary, and aren't his brothers James, Joseph, Simon and Judas? Aren't all his sisters with us? Where then did this man get all these things?" And they took offense at him (Mt 13:54-57).

By the time the credentials committee had finished its business, the congregation had most likely forgotten the content of Jesus' message.

In short, I don't think that we can entertain God's truth in our minds and hearts without acknowledging our inner poverty. How can the soul begin to fill with the truth of God's word until it experiences its own emptiness? We will not be able to hear God's word so long as our minds are scrambled with too many words of our own.

If I were called to be a prophet (an ambition which I do not have), my first condition would be that God guarantee the accuracy of my forecasts. I would insist that he second my denunciations with some well-aimed lightning and roof-splintering thunder. It would be terribly disconcerting to have God change his mind, as he did on Jonah. The only type of God I could comfortably work for would be a God of power and might to stand behind me with signs and wonders, a God whose voice would shake buildings and make cities tremble, a God whose fierce anger would strike terror into all the militarists, the greedy land barons, the loan sharks and extortionists of this world. Of course, these demands arise from the side of me that clamors for revenge, not the side that thirsts after justice. For there is something inside of us that enjoys licking wounds, rehearsing hurt feelings, and conjuring up gruesome punishments for the Idi Amins and Pol Pots, the gangsters and torturers of this world.

The story of Elijah on Mount Horeb intrigues me because it reveals such an astonishing perception of God. At least on that occasion, God showed himself to be a God of whispers, not a Lord of thunder and outrage:

> Then a great and powerful wind tore the mountains apart and shattered the rocks before the Lord, but the Lord was not in the wind. After the wind there was an earthquake, but the Lord was not in the earthquake. After the earthquake came a fire, but the Lord was not in the fire. And after the fire came a gentle whisper. When Elijah heard it, he pulled his cloak over his face and went out and stood at the mouth of the cave. Then a voice said to him, "What are you doing here, Elijah?" (1 Kgs 19:11-13).

Had most of us been the exhausted prophet fleeing from an enraged queen, God's question would have been utterly deflating. As things turned out, Jezebel eventually met her well-deserved fate. She was thrown from a window and devoured by a pack of dogs—that satisfies our sense of justice. But this information is reported in the Second Book of Kings. Elijah didn't live to read it.

Most of us are probably ill-suited to be prophets because we harbor too much anger, and as scripture says, "Man's anger does not bring about the righteous life that God desires" (Jas 1:20). We might succumb to the temptation to use God's word for our own purposes—to quench our indignation, to manipulate people into doing what we proposed, and to fashion both church and state to our private taste. We have so many words about so many things—about who is right and who is wrong, about what God really thinks, about where the world should be heading—that we might not be poor enough to know and preach the truth. God could easily ask us, should we ever climb his mountain, "What are *you* doing here?"

God whispers. When the human spirit distends itself in

shouting, contentious thoughts, anger, or fear, then its words and actions will not be able to communicate either God's judgment or God's comfort. The Letter of James expressed it nicely: Imitate the prophets for their patience. Truth springs from patience, and patience is born in the experience of inner poverty. The poor understand what it is like to wait for the Lord to speak, and perhaps to wait very long for the Lord to act.

# Interlude 2

The power of truth lies in the fact that we must accommodate ourselves to the truth; truth will not bend to please us. And that is how things are between us and God too.

The human mind is natively poor. If it wants to contemplate truth, the mind must work at finding truth. The human heart is poor. If it wants to rejoice in another's love, the heart must first work at giving love. We experience that poverty which describes the human condition when our minds become unsure and confused, when our hearts become frightened or lonely. Our souls are poor. If we seek God, we cannot have God on our terms; we have to approach God where God is.

To be a believer, to be in the truth, to be drawn by the Spirit of God, results in learning to see as God sees, to desire what God desires, to esteem what God esteems. The great mystery of Christian faith is that God wants to be where his creatures are. Christians, therefore, will want to do no less. Eventually they will find themselves turning toward the poor and oppressed, concerned about the problems of injustice and hunger, because it was into this world that Jesus came, and here is where Christians must discover their Lord.

Where is Jesus in today's world? Can we expect to know him without feeling a real solidarity with other men and women, growing sensitive to their poverty, their weakness, and their loneliness? God is present among people, and thus as the Spirit helps us to center our vision on God we should not be surprised at being awakened to a deep awareness that we belong to others; that all men and women are related to us. Turning poor means being drawn out of oneself toward concern and love for others. Many

Christians have struggled to learn this lesson; through their writing and their example, they can teach us a great deal about where Jesus is to be found.

# 3

# Who Are the Poor
# Who Will Be Saved?

One of the canon lawyers put Shibli to a kind of test by asking him how many silver coins one needed to possess in order to be obliged to contribute alms. He replied: "Do you want me to answer according to the practice of lawyers or according to the practice of God's destitute?"

Sharafuddin Maneri,
*The Hundred Letters*

Clement of Alexandria once wrote a short treatise for the rich Christians of his city in which he explained the proper attitude toward wealth. In the course of his essay he remarked that, when all is said and done, there is no such thing as private property because the whole universe is the property of God. This defines all human beings, rich and poor alike, to be God's tenants and stewards. He entitled his treatise, "Who Is the Rich Man That Is Saved?" taking his cue from the gospel text about how hard it will be for the rich to enter the kingdom of heaven. But if you recall the astonishment of the disciples at Jesus' remark, you may suspect with the disciples that a poor person's chances of salvation might not be that much better:

> Jesus looked around and said to his disciples, "How hard it is for the rich to enter the kingdom of God!" The disciples were amazed at his words. But Jesus said again, "Children, how hard it is to enter the kingdom of God! It is easier for a camel to go through the eye of a needle than for a rich man to enter the kingdom of

67

God." The disciples were even more amazed, and said to each other, "Who then can be saved?" (Mk 10:23-26).

Speaking for the others, Peter reminded Jesus what they had given up: "We have left everything to follow you!" And Clement observed that this could not have amounted to very much—a few hooks and nets, and maybe a boat. Apparently, Jesus expected people to renounce everything. Clement was bothered by this because clearly, he figured, such a practice was socially and economically unworkable. Who would be left to support the poor and thereby to fulfill the Lord's commands about feeding the hungry and clothing the naked? The solution, according to Clement, was to use one's wealth as if one did not own it. But if this solution was to be more than merely pretending—"I am rich but I shall live as if I were not"—then Jesus would have to show his disciples how to crawl through the needle's eye.

In the last chapter I attempted to show how poverty touches every human being, whether or not one has enjoyed material prosperity. By that account, we may all look poor enough in God's sight to qualify for admission to the kingdom. But how does the truth of poverty become real and operative in our planning and living from day to day? Perhaps Clement had a capitalist point in the back of his mind. The outright renunciation of property (for which there are numerous outstanding Christian witnesses) would not eliminate material poverty, and sooner or later the world's resources would again concentrate in the hands of those who are shrewder and more industrious than their fellows. Thus the difficulty of determining how much to give and in what ways to give it remains. A burden rests across the shoulders of those who have both money and faith; the burden will not disappear.

It seems to me that the most accurate measure by which to assess the sincerity of one's efforts to deal with that burden is lifestyle. The manner in which people live either diminishes or increases their awareness of the evil living conditions, the hunger and injustice, the powerlessness and deprivation, which much of the world endures. Christians cannot discharge their stewardship just by making donations; there is the further matter of learning to see the poor as sisters and brothers and of living with the awareness that the poor belong to us and we belong to the poor. Our salvation depends on this.

The basic issue, therefore, is lifestyle, and in this chapter I want to develop an example that illumines how we who are rich learn to follow a Christ who is poor.

In the fifth chapter of its *Dogmatic Constitution on the Church*, the Second Vatican Council wrote that "all the faithful of Christ of whatever rank or status are called to the fullness of the Christian life and to the perfection of charity . . . one and the same holiness is cultivated by all who are moved by the Spirit of God." By reason of their baptism all Christians share the same dignity, equality, and call to holiness. Although most of us did not make our baptismal profession personally (our parents or godparents spoke on our behalf), we have ratified our baptismal promises many times over the years by taking part in the Eucharist. In assenting to those promises we indicated our willingness to live according to the gospel.

Every Christian life, therefore, becomes evangelical. Each Christian's life unfolds a more or less clearly formulated desire to follow Jesus and to associate with others who also confess Jesus to be their way, their truth, and their life. While the shape of each life differs in its particulars, the general pattern of living which the gospel dictates should be discernible in all of us: prayer, purity of heart, selfless love of neighbor, dedication to the kingdom of God and his justice, and a daily effort to discover the freedom and joy of joining the ranks of God's poor. No Christian can pledge to do more than to live out the gospel wholeheartedly; the obligation which we accept at baptism and reaffirm at the Eucharist cannot be improved on. The invitation to follow Christ comes to all alike.

How then do we defend those who embrace religious life in the formal sense of belonging to a community which pronounces vows of poverty, chastity, and obedience? In view of the fact that their numbers have been decreasing over the last few decades, this may be a timely question. If all Christians are asked to be perfect in living out the gospel, then the baptismal promises cannot be outdone even by the religious vows. Otherwise, there would be a "gospel within the gospel" which some Christians are permitted to hear for the sake of a "more perfect" following of Christ.

The difficulty over religious life has been settled in recent years through a renewed appreciation for the variety of gifts and talents planted among us by the Spirit for the building up of the body of Christ. No graces are given without regard for the needs of the whole church. Grace is shared, not as a personal privilege to be privately contemplated and enjoyed, but for the sake of knitting the entire people of God more closely in faith, in holiness, and in charity. This rule of grace applies to religious life, to married couples, and to people who decide to remain single. We depend on one another's gifts, insight into the gospel, and dedication to God's truth.

Nevertheless, religious life has something to teach the rest of the church, and the world too, about how to be human. As a specific lifestyle adopted by some Christians, religious life illustrates the consequences of one's baptismal profession. When people observe religious life zealously and earnestly, they dramatize the pattern of evangelical living which all Christians should be embodying in their lives. Just as the eucharistic liturgy dramatically and symbolically intensifies what every life should be—prayerful, sacrificial, and God-centered—so also the religious life intensifies for the whole community what each lifestyle ought to be—simple, clean-souled, and earnest about seeking and doing God's will.

Religious life has assumed many forms throughout the church's history. Men and women have abandoned the world for barren desert hermitages, served feverishly in the midst of the world's slums, or enclosed themselves behind convent walls in contemplative silence. Oddly enough, the solitary life represents a particularly dramatic manner of living out one's baptism. But the urge to retreat into one's inner space is by no means an exclusively religious or monastic concern. Most of us want time to think and pray over those occasional experiences which reveal where we came from and where we are going. Only a few people will express their need for silence by means of a solitary quest for communion with the Spirit who calls from the depths of the human heart. But their lifestyle is a beacon of grace which throws our own desires into relief as we climb our way on an equally arduous, though less spectacular, ascent toward the God who is creating us.

The best description of the nature of monastic solitude has been given, I think, by Thomas Merton in his essay, "Notes for a Philosophy of Solitude." Like so many of his writings, that essay is also relevant to Christians who do not live within a monastic enclosure. The solitary life, as Merton drew its picture, is a form of Christian living which instructs us about the connection between being human and being religious. The central piece of this instruction is the person of Christ.

### A Brief Word About the Basic Doctrine

A historical overview of the church's teaching about Jesus would disclose two basic convictions. First, unless Jesus is completely human, then God's salvation has not touched human beings. And second, unless Jesus is truly God's Son, then his ministry—the life, teachings, and signs, the death and resurrection of Jesus—has no power to

71

liberate us. In the man Jesus, God reaffirmed the nobility and highest possibility of human nature, that we do in fact come from God and that we have the capacity to share God's own life. In Jesus, the Lord and Christ, the living God heals our brokenness and restores our power to trust God's providential care of the world. Our only access to understanding what Christ's divinity means is through meditation on his humanness. And Jesus as God's Son, the Word made flesh, is the brightest expression of what being human means.

The Christian's experience and understanding of God depends upon the humanity of Jesus as it is portrayed in the gospels. Throughout the centuries, Christians have felt free to use their imaginations in re-creating the gospel scenes in order to speak with Jesus as they contemplated the events of his ministry. Christians have not regarded Jesus as a means to God which can be placed alongside other figures from the world's great religions. The humanity of Christ states what God is truly like. As the early church writers would have explained, since men and women have been fashioned in the image of God, and Christ is the divine likeness, then the human heart needs to become Christian if it is to realize its highest potential.

In trying to help someone understand who Jesus is, it is important to bear in mind the difference between the way of doctrine and the way of discipleship. The creeds and doctrines of the church state clearly what our understanding of Jesus is; we would not preach about him or proclaim him to be our personal Lord and Savior unless we believed him to be God's Son. But the way of discipleship is the way of experience. Only by attempting to follow Jesus, by struggling to remain faithful to God and to deal with personal sinfulness, will we ever come to understand what the church's doctrine means. Each Christian needs to retrace the steps of the original disciples by which they also grew in their knowledge of who Jesus was and what he had done. The solitary life sheds much light on the way of discipleship.

## What the Solitary Life Expresses

Imagine the solitary person to be one who has withdrawn from the world in order to pursue a path of silent, vigilant, and patient attention to the God who speaks from within the human heart and who has spoken in an unsurpassable way in the heart of Jesus Christ. Imagine further that the solitary person's life is religious in the formal sense of being poor, chaste, and obedient. To the degree that he or she actually lives out the gospel, and not the counterfeit apartness of a recluse, this person bears witness to the baptismal promise to follow Jesus which every Christian makes. Let me explain why.

On one level, the solitary person simply appears to be someone who has renounced the world, putting a distance between the daily concerns of ordinary men and women and a freshly awakened love for the kingdom of God. The solitary person lays aside action in favor of contemplation, preferring Mary's lead over Martha's (Lk 10:38-42).

But the desire for solitude, human though it is, can be fulfilled authentically or inauthentically. It is fulfilled authentically when someone seeks God selflessly in order to be in a steady communion with him. The desire is fulfilled inauthentically when solitude becomes a flight from the world, an escape from the care for others and the personal relationships which our being human requires. Withdrawal from the world turns into escape when one retreats to inner space in order to avoid responsibility for the lives of others. Running away diminishes our capacity for real communion. There is also an inauthentic way of being with others. People can be used to fill up our own emptiness when we want them around but without the risk of letting their lives touch ours, when we have neither the time nor the genuine affection to let them share their inner experience with us.

When solitude is authentic, our capacity for communion grows as the inward journey approaches God. Why? Because God also has concerns, and we cannot be with God for very long without sharing in what is of concern to him. Always present to the God whom Christians experience are the people whom God calls to life and for whom he cares. The great marvel about the solitary person is his heightened awareness of the yearning of the whole human race for God. Thus, the solitary person is soon joined to the rest of the world by the intensity of her desire and prayer on behalf of others. The solitary person dramatizes a universal quest for what is life-giving, and his experience proves that the way to communion with others cannot bypass solitude, that personal desert marked out for each of us by the finger of God, as Merton put it. But by embracing solitude and the soul's thirst for God, one uncovers the resources for true and lasting solidarity with the world. For Christians, there is a spiritual law which holds that God cannot be found in spite of or apart from his creatures; God meets us in and through his works. A Christian cannot simply "renounce" the world.

The history of Christian piety records some painful episodes about believers who regarded the things which God created and pronounced good as stumbling blocks to holiness. All Christians, whether solitary or not, are supposed to avoid temptation. But a religion which preaches the Incarnation resists any suggestion that the world itself is one great temptation. Neither material things, nor sexual fulfillment, nor the free and responsible pursuit of one's ideals, can be evil. Therefore, what is the point of giving up these things? What sort of witness would the solitary person present to the larger community of believers if her lifestyle implied that creatures must be circumvented in the "more perfect" search for the kingdom of God?

From one viewpoint, then, through the vows of poverty, chastity, and obedience, the solitary person has embraced three evils. Poverty destroys the possibility of genuine human development; it is the scourge of the Third World and a growing specter even among the affluent nations. It doesn't help matters to argue that the profession of poverty testifies to evangelical detachment, because the gospel obliges all of Christ's followers to a proper use of creatures and to live as stewards of the goods entrusted to our care. In fact, to some Christians detachment might look like a spiritual luxury. It is difficult for those who labor hard to raise and support their families to appreciate the professional detachment of religious people.

The same reasoning applies to celibacy and obedience. The celibate renounces marriage, sexual relationships, and both the burdens and joys of family life. Obedience involves the radical curtailment of personal ambition by subordinating oneself to the will of another. To depart in this way from normal human aspirations is to choose a way of living that most people would legitimately think of as strange.

Furthermore, the suggestion that any Christian life could be either exclusively active or exclusively contemplative misrepresents the gospel. Jesus' own example of prayer integrated into an active public ministry suggests instead that Christian action is not possible without personal, solitary prayer. It likewise suggests that Christian prayer is by its nature communal, no matter how solitary its practice. While Jesus told his disciples to enter their rooms and pray to the Father in private, he also instructed them to say "our" Father (Mt 6:5-15). And as some scripture scholars have noted, there is also some significance to the fact that Luke juxtaposed the story of Martha and Mary with the story of the Good Samaritan (Lk 10:25-37, 38-42). One would have expected Jesus, in light of the preceding verses, to ask Mary to be a "good samaritan" and assist her sister in preparing the meal. But Luke's organization may be hinting that genuine worship of God does not take place in the Temple; it occurs through service of one's neighbor. And real Christian service calls for contemplative attention to the words of Christ rather than cooking food for hungry guests.

The solitary life, therefore, is not the pure pursuit of contemplation for its own sake. Without concern for the neighbor, prayer is not Christian. And since all Christians are enjoined to pray, even ceaselessly (1 Thes 5:17), how would the solitary person's life of prayer be an example for the rest of God's people if his or her practice of prayer neglected the neighbor? I think that this question pushes us to look at the solitary life on a second, deeper level.

### The Christian Pattern of Life

The gospels picture Jesus as teaching and exemplifying the sort of existence appropriate to one who is living between the kingdom of God inaugurated and the kingdom of God yet to come. The world, in other words, has not yet taken on the shape that God intends for it. Anyone who responds to Jesus' call to discipleship will have to imitate the manner of life Jesus leads: a life of total trust in God (Lk 12:22-26), of selfless service to others (Jn 15:9-17), a life rich in the joy of seeing others come to faith (Mt 11:25-26), a life which takes up the cross yet discovers the burden to be light (Mt 11:28-30). The solitary life represents the gospel in a dramatic fashion. It accents the single-minded pursuit of God's kingdom through prayer and self-denial. Through its deep trust in God, the solitary life throws into relief the fact that all human beings are pilgrims on the earth. So eager is the solitary person to establish the kingdom on earth, when God's will shall prevail in the hearts and minds of all men and women, that he brooks no compromise with his love for that real treasure (Lk 14:25-35). Because her capacity for loving is centered on God's kingdom, her prayer is drawn profoundly toward desiring and respecting God's designs for the world's future.

On this level, the religious observance of poverty,

chastity, and obedience does not take on the appearance of being an exceptional example of life according to the gospel. Instead, it intensifies the pattern of Christian discipleship in order to make public those elements of discipleship which every Christian life should embody. Every Christian life, and each Christian community, should be witnessing to the fact that the reign of God has begun but still awaits its final form. Even if most Christians do not dramatize the gospel as the solitary person does, still, each of our lives can be dramatic in terms of our particular translation of Christ's teaching and example. When faith is alive and people are living in the Lord's presence, poverty is not so much what is promised as what people become, namely, God-possessed and not self-possessed. Obedience is not so much what is promised as what they become, namely, listeners-in-faith. And chastity is not so much the promise of bodily purity as what people become, namely, a living hope that God's kingdom which has not been fully realized on the earth is worth waiting for with an absolute dedication.

The solitary person, therefore, conforms his or her life to the example of Jesus. This ideal is not restricted, however, to those few souls who feel capable of being perfect. Patterning one's life after the example of Jesus is a gospel ideal, and so it belongs to all Christians. The problem which needs to be faced is that none of us imitates Jesus' example without considerable personal cost. Between the pattern and its successful translation into our lives there needs to occur some inner transformation that makes us want to be disciples of Christ, eager to be identified as his companions, and capable of following in his footsteps. Between Jesus as teacher and Jesus as example there stands Jesus as savior, the one who frees people to be with him so that God's concerns can rule their hearts.

*Identifying With the World and Identifying With Jesus*
I have been proposing that the religious vows pledge

the solitary person to living in a manner which many people might look upon as strange, even as contrary to God's plan. But the evil which a solitary person accepts is not unlike the evil of the crucifixion, where defeat is overturned in the great Christian symbol of victory and life.

The solitary person adopts an austere lifestyle, freely. But would it be too much to perceive in this free choice a desire to identify with those fellow human beings who are poor, but not by choice? The vow of poverty provides a way of identifying with, and remaining permanently mindful of, those who are victims of injustice, unwanted, deprived of opportunities, or imprisoned in their destitution. Through voluntary poverty the solitary person wants to touch the brokenness and alienation which many human beings endure—both the marginal people of the world and those who are poor in courage, companionship, and hope; those, in other words, who may be materially rich but have suffered the loss of what truly matters.

Likewise, the solitary person undertakes a lifestyle which precludes the fulfillment of some normal human aspirations. Would it be extreme to suggest that the solitary person has chosen to identify with those people in the world who will never reach perfect human fulfillment, not by their own choice but through the finger of bad fortune? Celibacy and obedience commit the solitary person to being one with the crippled, the handicapped, those who have no voice over their own futures, those who lie forgotten in prisons and hospitals, those whom painful experiences have made incapable of sustaining a lasting relationship, those who have discovered that there is no perfect marriage, no perfect friendship, no perfect anything in this life.

Through these vows, the solitary person comes to share the concerns of God. Instead of renouncing personal responsibility, one freely lays one's life in the hands of another in order to dramatize a mystery about human existence: All of us are creatures and no one is sovereign over

78

his or her life. The solitary person has not renounced the
world after all; he wears it by identifying personally and
perpetually with its estrangement, its poverty and failure,
its loneliness and sin. Poverty, chastity, and obedience are
the traits of a liberated soul; they signify the solitary
person's solidarity with the suffering and the hope of the
wider human family.

I am afraid that someone will charge me with being
romantic about the solitary lifestyle, an accusation which
would have some ground if this account is divorced from
the person of Christ. The great Christian fact is that God has
entered the human condition; in becoming flesh, God identified himself with the fortunes of a sinful humanity. His
company consisted of the broken people of the earth: He
joined the religious and cultural history of a small, oppressed race; he lived among the poor and deprived, the sick
and diseased; he struck up friendships with sinners. His mission was to be the bearer of good news for the poor: "I must
preach the good news of the kingdom of God to the other
towns also, because that is why I was sent" (Lk 4:43). Even
in death he had criminals for companions (Lk 23:32). The
great Christian fact, then, is that God has expressed his
solidarity with the world through the incarnation of his
Word, the one whose name had to be Emmanuel, God-with-
us (Mt 1:23). In assuming our flesh, Christ also put on the
burden of our condition, but by doing so he showed us how
real is God's desire to reconcile the world, to heal it, to bind
its sores, and through this close identification with us, to
draw all things to himself (Jn 12:32). By identifying with and
embracing the broken world, Jesus heals it and lifts it up.

The solitary person demonstrates an identification with
the world by reason of her desire to identify with Jesus. Paul
had urged his converts to imitate his manner of living out
the gospel just as he imitated Christ (1 Cor 11:1), and just as
Christ imitated the Father (Jn 5:19-20). For those trying to
live according to the gospel, the desire to imitate Jesus leads

to a solidarity with the people Jesus came to save. While the solitary person dramatizes this mystery, by accepting the gospel at our baptism all of us Christians have committed ourselves to living out the deep mystery of God's union with a sinful world. We might even say that the solitary person helps us to see what it means to imitate God.

## From Teacher to Savior

It is fairly easy to accept Jesus as a teacher who instructs his disciples about how to live, or as a model of the life of faith which they are supposed to imitate. But Jesus is also the savior who sets them free to follow his example. Consequently, there needs to be a third level in our reflection on the solitary life. Through the power of his death and resurrection and the gift of his Spirit, Jesus enables the disciples to be in his company.

In his work *On Spiritual Knowledge,* the fifth-century Eastern saint, Diadochos of Photiki, made an insightful observation about the obligation of the rich to give to the poor. Once the rich have dispossessed themselves of their wealth, they might resent the fact that they can no longer give to the poor, not out of special affection for those who are needy, but because of the sour taste that financial powerlessness leaves in their soul. Diadochos writes:

> The Lord will demand from us an account of our help to the needy according to what we have and not according to what we have not. If, then, from fear of God I distribute in a short space of time what I might have given away over many years, on what grounds can I be accused, seeing that I now have nothing? On the other hand, it might be argued: "Who now will give help to the needy that depend on regular gifts out of my modest means?" A person who argues in this way must learn not to insult God because of his own love of money. God will not fail to provide for his own

creation as he has done from the beginning; for before this or that person was prompted to give help, the needy did not lack food or clothing. Understanding this we should reject, in a spirit of true service, the senseless presumption which arises from wealth and we should hate our own desires—which is to hate our own soul. Then, no longer possessing wealth which we enjoy distributing, we shall begin to feel our worthlessness intensely, because we cannot now perform any good works. Certainly, provided there is some good in us, we gladly obey the divine command and as long as we are well off, we enjoy giving things away. But when we have exhausted everything, an ill-defined gloom and a sense of abasement come over us, because we think we are doing nothing worthy of God's righteousness.

The effect of this realization brings the soul to a new stage of self-knowledge and its complete dependence upon God:

In this deep abasement the soul returns to itself, so as to procure through the labor of prayer, through patience and humility what it can no longer acquire by the daily giving of help to the needy.

This text is marvelously sensitive to the spiritual difficulty which the solitary life uncovers so clearly. The solitary person learns that his or her identifying with the world was not a condescending gesture; he did not lower himself in order to have some share in the human condition. The solitary person does not graciously assume the world's brokenness, but rather (as Merton remarked) she discovers the sinfulness of the world inside herself. In experiencing his own rupture of soul, he longs for the healing presence of God.

The path to salvation never sidesteps the human predicament; it passes directly through the world's weakness, and involves being nailed to that weakness along the way. This is what the solitary person comes to understand. Out of a purified faith and a humbled love, the solitary person approaches Christ in order to be saved, to be liberated in order to follow Christ closely, and to have his or her capacity for loving others set loose, to taste the deep human need for inner healing, to feel with God the hurt, the loneliness, and the anguished struggle of the human race for peace.

The religious vows do not impose on the solitary life a fresh burden, as it were, from the outside. On the contrary, the vows are accurate statements of real personal poverty, of real personal inability to have a final determination over one's life, and of real personal inadequacy in one's affection for others. By acknowledging these human marks, the solitary person achieves genuine solidarity with the world and appreciates Christ's solidarity with us. The solitary person gives a dramatic illustration of these basic features of human life. By entering his or her inner space to find God in prayer and silence, the solitary person owns up to a deep unworthiness: "Go away from me, Lord, I am a sinful man!"

Poverty, chastity, and obedience help the church to see what redeemed existence means; they are the trademarks of life according to the gospel. All Christians are called upon to unite themselves with the Christ who joined himself to a broken world. Their sensitivity to the world's many hungers and their union with the world's poor is the other side of their union with Christ. In the solitary lifestyle, the rhythm of redeemed existence is dramatically enacted. The solitary life illumines the church's central belief about Jesus Christ and the intimate connection between who he is and what he has done for us. The way of discipleship is the way of experience, for through experience the disciple understands why Jesus is not only teacher and model, but savior.

## Conclusion

I began this chapter by asking who the poor are who need to be saved. By now the answer ought to be clear: Those poor are each of us.

The humanity of Jesus anchors our faith in God's solidarity with a world waiting to be liberated, and the divinity of Jesus anchors our belief that because of God's solidarity with us, our power to believe, to trust, and to love has been set free. Maybe that is why Jesus told his disciples:

> "And if I go and prepare a place for you, I will come back and take you to be with me that you also may be where I am" (Jn 14:3).

"That you may be where I am": But where is Jesus now, and how do we even now go about being where he is? The Word came to dwell among us in order that we might live in the presence of the Word.

Every believer (not just monks) lives a portion of the solitary life. In baptism, we declare the events of Jesus' life to be the guiding points for our life. By aligning our future to his, we are implicating ourselves in the future of all men and women. The day comes when we discover how we carry the human condition inside our very selves, revealed in our own hopes and desires, our inner poverty and alienation. As teacher and model, Jesus shows us how to be human. But as savior, Jesus reaches out to heal our fearful souls and rebuild our weakened faith. "Take courage! It is I. Don't be afraid" (Mk 6:50).

The Spirit of Jesus makes it possible for human beings to be religious; the Spirit enables us to recognize how our inner poverty unites us to our brothers and sisters all over the world. For we need to be kept aware of God's concerns, and the concerns of God are global. The solitary life, by its prayerful style and its formal profession of poverty, chasti-

83

ty, and obedience, stands as a steady witness to these great Christian facts. It represents perfection, not by abstracting itself from the larger community of faith, but by illustrating life according to the gospel, which is perfect because Jesus, God's word and grace to us, lived it.

# Interlude 3

In his commentary on the prophets, Abraham Heschel suggested that there are two basic forms in which the prophet expresses sympathy. First, the prophet feels with God, that is, he feels what God is experiencing. Secondly, the prophet feels for God, that is, his feelings are aroused because of what God is going through. The prophet's outrage over injustice and religious abuse reveals the nature and intensity of divine feeling. God himself grows angry and outraged over his people, and the prophet lets them know it. But the prophet also shows sympathy for God. He feels badly because God is having such a difficult time with his stiff-necked creatures, or the prophet feels confident and hopeful because God has been moved to pity and love.

The prophet might be defined, following Heschel's suggestion, as someone who has shared in God's experience. This participation so aggravates his or her existence that the prophet's life calls dramatic attention to the way God experiences the world. Indeed, prophets bear witness to intensely religious feeling, often to the extent of laying down their lives. But I would call such people prophets and not only martyrs for their faith because they demonstrate what happens to a human life which has been overcome by sympathy with and for the Lord. That is what makes the words of an Amos or Hosea so memorable, or the frustration of Jonah so touchingly comical. That is what draws us back to texts like these:

> "Can a mother forget the baby at
>     her breast
> and have no compassion on the
>     child she has borne?
> Though she may forget,

I will not forget you!
See, I have engraved you on the
    palms of my hands" (Is 49:15-16).

"As a mother comforts her child,
so will I comfort you" (66:13).

Perhaps we don't learn enough from the prophets because we become distracted by the dramatic side of their witness and fail to notice what God is like for them. I believe that there are genuine prophets roaming the world, most of them probably hidden from our view. They experience in their own souls both the range of God's feeling for the world and the deep poverty of those who suffer. Whether they would say so or not, their feeling for God is like the feeling one friend has for another.

In addition to prophets, there are lovers. These are men and women whose lives might be described as stories of being in love with God. Some would call such people mystics, but the word "mystic" conjures up too many fuzzy notions about God. Great mystery surrounds God, but there is nothing intrinsically obscure about God. Mystics have been known to talk about a certain darkness which covers the soul and its thoughts as an individual ascends the holy mountain which is the divine presence. But as far as I can tell, the only meaningful trait that adequately describes the experience which mystics have is love; and so I shall refer to them as lovers. They are madly in love with God, and they have found out that God is madly in love with them. Their hearts have no other desire than to be possessed by the love they can neither explain nor control. Their lives become aggravated by desire; they would be willing to part with everything for God's sake.

While most of us become confused and unclear about what exactly we really want, what we are really living for, the lover leaves no doubt that clearly and simply there is only one love which matters. That is not to say that they ig-

86

nore their neighbors, or that they devote themselves to serving their brothers and sisters only to prove their love for God. For God is not another person alongside everyone else. God is the sacred presence which pervades everything we do, touch, think about, and hope for. The lover does not love a God who competes with human beings for affection, nor does the lover reduce other human beings to means by which love for God is demonstrated. God is altogether different. God is what a person knows from being fully in love. The "object" of that love is personal; it is pervasive; it is all-embracing. It is personal without being absorbed by one individual being—not even by a being that is supreme. It is pervasive and is not turned on and off, depending on the lover's mood. It is all-embracing, incapable of being restricted only to certain people. The lover knows neither enemies nor strangers, only friends; indeed, the lover knows only sisters and brothers.

Finally, there are the pilgrims. Real lovers exist, just as there are real prophets; but most of us are not such thoroughgoing lovers that our lives become dramatic expressions of being in love with God. And so we would probably prefer to portray the situation in which we find ourselves in a humbler way. Most of us are pilgrims, men and women slowly making their way along a journey of faith. We love, but our love is in need of much growing up and purifying. We trust God, but not with that unshakable confidence that comes from having known how deeply God loves us. We bear witness to the religious values we cherish, but without the intensity and single-mindedness of the prophetic witness. We are pilgrims. And like pilgrims down through the centuries, we follow an inner map which leads to the discovery of what we really are, to a place in our own souls made sacred by the Spirit's presence.

# 4

# Traveling Home

There were shacks all over these hills, in the most unlikely places, built against boulders and cave entrances, and at the bottom of sand pits. I came to fear them, because at each one there was a mangy dog that ran out and yapped at me, snarling into its paws. I was genuinely frightened of being bitten by one of these mutts: they had a crazy rabid look, and a bark from one excited barks from other dogs hidden all over the stony hillside. Giving these dogs a wide berth, I strayed from the mule tracks. . . . I mentioned the dogs to a Colombian that evening. There seemed to be a lot of mutts in the hills, I said. Were they dangerous? "*Some* of the dogs are dangerous," he said. "But *all* the snakes are deadly poisonous." "I did not see any snakes." "Maybe not. But they saw you."

Paul Theroux,
*The Old Patagonian Express*

"Happy folk are Hobbits to dwell near the shores of the sea!" said Haldir. "It is long indeed since any of my folk have looked on it, yet still we remember it in song. Tell me of these havens as we walk." "I cannot," said Merry, "I have never seen them. I have never been out of my own land before. And if I had known what the world outside was like, I don't think I should have the heart to leave it."

J. R. R. Tolkien,
*The Lord of the Rings*

A good traveler's tale makes exciting reading. Through imagination we board ships, arrive on railway platforms, await the takeoff of giant aircraft, or start hiking in the wilderness. We traverse oceans and continents, raft down uncharted rivers, visit remote monasteries and temples, wind through Oriental bazaars or join camel caravans, taste exotic fruits, sip coffee under a bedouin's tent in the Sinai Desert, bargain with Sikhs over precious carpets in the Kashmir, trek through the foothills of the Himalayas, or get stranded by a road-erasing typhoon. The tale might include a tiger or two, moments of intense personal enlightenment, narrow escapes, or haunting legends.

People travel, or want to travel, for a variety of reasons. For some, travel spells adventure, new experiences, a broadening of horizon. Geography and history, space and time, come alive at China's Great Wall, or the massive Buddhist shrine at Borobudur in Indonesia, or on the Mount of Olives overlooking Jerusalem. There is great personal satisfaction in getting close to such places. For others, travel simply provides an enviable way to take a vacation. Provided the fare is right, it makes little difference to them where they go. Getting away, being on the road and away from dreary routine, is all that matters.

For still others (and I count myself among them), travel has a lot to do with the need of making a journey. The opportunity to travel enables us to live out—perhaps to act out—the intuition that life itself is a journey. Traveling becomes a parable about human existence; it expresses an inner moment in one's experience of being human. The experienced traveler knows how unwise and unnecessary it is to bring along much luggage. You escape the worry of fetching it, checking it in and out of customs stations, carrying it, and often guarding it. Some instinct in you wants to prove that you can survive with fewer possessions, and by setting out with just a few basic items, you discover the refreshing freedom of the seasoned traveler. Such is the freedom which comes from turning poor.

The journey motif has been strong in Western literature. I still remember daydreaming my way one sum-

mer during high school through the *Iliad* and the *Odyssey* of
Homer. That led into Vergil's *Aeneid,* Chaucer's *Canter-
bury Tales,* Dante's *Divine Comedy,* and the quest for the
Holy Grail from the legend of King Arthur. All the world
was making a journey, I mused; what about me? My sense
of journeying and being on some important adventure was
revived when, 25 years later, I discovered *The Lord of the
Rings.*

But there was also Thomas Merton's *Seven Storey
Mountain* and *The Long Loneliness* by Dorothy Day. Those
lives helped to put many Christians in touch with elements
of their own pilgrimage through life. Pilgrimage is an appropriate word too. Human life is a pilgrimage to the extent
that we sense ourselves heading somewhere, leaving places
where we have already set our mark and taking along with
us the collected souvenirs of any life journey, our memories
and our relationships.

Travel tales tend to be crisper than autobiographies, I
think, because the traveler tells of definite points of landing
and departure. We can visualize the takeoff and return, the
setting out and coming home. But the contours of a life
journey may be less clearly defined. Our origins are clouded
in mists that we shall never see through, while our ultimate
destination gets shrouded by the gnawing uncertainty of
graveyards. Perhaps the urge to travel symbolizes a need to
find out about our life journey, where we really came from
and where we are really heading. Or it may reflect deep-
seated fear which pulls us away from a confrontation with
the only journey that matters—the journey into the silent
stirrings of one's heart—by setting us constantly on the
move, pretending to ourselves that we have actually
covered some distance.

Journeys, at any rate, have their spiritual side. They
dramatize life experience and draw clear points of origin and
arrival on the matrix of life. But life is a unique sort of
journey; it may take us a long time to clarify and resolve the

inner puzzles of our experience: What makes us want to set out, to be on the road, to be heading toward something or someplace? What attracts us into reading about the travels and pilgrimages which other people have made? What are the signs that we have made some progress?

There are times when I feel as if my life were in an hourglass, and whenever I notice the slow falling of the sand, my insides cave in with apprehension. I want to stop the grains from slipping through the funnel. The prospect of going somewhere, of charting a new goal for myself, seems to turn the hourglass around and wins for me a new lease on time. But what fresh answers will the new journeying bring, and why do I become anxious about the passing of time, which cannot be reversed no matter how daring the journey? One has to learn, I suppose, that traveling the world, like hiking a backwoods trail, may disguise a deep uncertainty about the human condition, an inability to settle down and encounter the mystery which human existence throws at us. Of course, many people never set foot out of familiar territory for fear of getting lost, or of suffering the misfortunes which sometimes befall the traveler. But there can be no avoiding the fact that every one of us is a fellow pilgrim in the world. The whole human race has embarked upon a journey; its history will some day be told as one immense traveler's tale.

Traveling is more enjoyable, I found, if you have a companion, a friend with whom you talk over the trip, make plans, and share memories later on. You might dare a few more exploits, visit places you would be afraid to enter alone, or sample strange foods. So too with inner journeying: It helps to have friends. And what do you learn from these travels? Journeying teaches, I think, that one can never attain perfect clarity about life and the final reason why things are the way they are. Life takes so many unexpected turns; it demands adjusting our plans, changing our routes, living with occasional cancellations. The tale of a life journey borrows upon elements of faith, intuitions rather than firm conclusions. Its course depends upon what has happened to us, what we paused to take a closer look at, what kind of people we met along the way. What we eventually come to think about life may be more, or it may be less, than what our neighbors and fellow pilgrims were able to believe in.

Inner geography has its own kind of space and time, its own moments of setting out and coming home. The outer geography of the universe is relative to inner space. After one long, steady look at a sky full of stars, who would not suspect a connection between searching for a goal which remains unattainable and the urge to be on a journey? The incredibly vast distances between star systems simply dwarf by comparison any earthly voyage. If anyone has trouble finding his or her proper place on the earth, what hope will there be of coming to feel at home in the cosmos? Perhaps it is impossible for human beings to develop an at-homeness in the world because we are only pilgrims. But if we were to locate our rightful position in the arrangement of the cosmos, then we would have reached the center of things, that point where all journeying consciously or unconsciously heads. Without crossing interstellar distances, we would have discovered the dimensions of inner space which lend proportion and meaning to the universe. We would have entered the theory of relativity with a vengeance.

Restlessness, that profound uncertainty in our souls which yearns for an assurance of our importance and place in the universe, will persist among human beings from one age to the next. But we have only faith to fall back on. Or rather, we experience a number of forces working in our life which seem to draw faith out of us. Without such experience—without uncertainty, anxiety, restlessness, and soul-searching—faith would not be genuine. Faith becomes substantial—it is tempered and fortified—through fear and risk. Who, like Peter, would not sink the first time he attempted walking toward God over the waves?

## Desire and Call

The journey motif is pronounced in religious literature, particularly, of course, in the books of the Bible. But equally remarkable, I think, is the theme of a spiritual call. By means of angels, heavenly voices, or unusual events and encounters, God brought people either to a new way of life or to some special work, or to deeper prayer. Scripture records how Abraham listened to God's voice directing him to set out on a journey:

> The Lord said to Abram, "Leave your country, your people and your father's household and go to the land I will show you" (Gn 12:1).

Jacob had a dream at Bethel in which he was invited to put his trust in the Lord:

> "I am with you and will watch over you wherever you go, and I will bring you back to this land. I will not leave you until I have done what I promised you." When Jacob awoke from his sleep, he thought, "Surely the Lord was in this place, and I was not aware of it" (Gn 28:15-16).

Trusting in this God would not be easy, as Jacob learned after a night's struggle with a divine stranger:

> Then the man said, "Your name will no longer be Jacob but Israel, because you have struggled with God and with men and have overcome" (Gn 32:28).

To be called to trust entails being called to wrestle with the strangeness of God's ways.

Jonah was called to preach a mission in Niniveh, and God had to enlist the services of a great fish to deliver him there. In the tenth chapter of the Acts of the Apostles, we read that Peter went to Cornelius' house after a vision of food, like a picnic blanket dropping from the sky, and in the 13th chapter Luke tells us how the Spirit guided the early church at Antioch to let Saul and Barnabas be free for apostolic travel. The sight of diseased, wrinkled, and dead men moved the young Siddhartha to embrace a life of contemplation; this was his call to become the Buddha, the enlightened one. And the same sort of misery led Mother Teresa to give up teaching in order to care for the dying people of the Calcutta streets.

The story of each person's call will be told differently because each one's call is composed of circumstances which are uniquely his or hers. Heavy traces of divine providence can be found in the particular times and places, the backgrounds and personalities, the geographies and cultures in which the calling took place. Abraham wandered in the ancient Near East, the Buddha meditated in the foothills of the Himalayas, Thomas Merton found himself in a monastery in Kentucky, Dorothy Day set up shelters for the poor and jobless in New York. The call is heard within the dimensions of one's inner space. People are changed as a result of their call; their lives become inseparable from the experience of that call and their new experience of God. Sebastian Moore pointed out that we do not view God the same way before and after the death of a loved one, or before and after the death of Jesus. Neither do we regard him the same way before and after being challenged to leave our familiar ground and aim for something new.

Because I singled out as examples people whose lives and contributions appear gigantic next to ours, I am not implying that God calls only giants—or, since we only know about his grace after the stories are told, that God calls individuals only when he has a major project in mind. Reading about Abraham and Jacob, Ruth and Esther, or Dorothy Day and Oscar Romero is not supposed to make us feel insignificant by comparison, nor even to confirm a suspicion that God intervenes in history every now and then. These people did lead outstanding lives. But so do countless others who raise families, practice and hand on the faith, and share God's concerns. The pioneers are models who dramatize the "lines of spiritual motion," as Flannery O'Connor termed the movements of grace. The pioneers do not serve a higher divine purpose, simply a different one.

God calls to each of us, though I would be hard pressed to explain to anyone how this happens. People cannot be told *how* God is speaking to them; they can only be assured *that* God speaks. It would be too easy to slip from how God speaks to what he is saying, and therefore, to what others should be hearing. But it seems to me that each of us wants to be called and wants to believe that God is interested enough in each of us personally to demonstrate some sign of his affection and care. One loud, universal call delivered to the whole world by a divine address system would not be very compelling. That kind of call would be too general and too easily ignored. In fact, however, God only speaks out of the concrete images and events of daily life. We are not equipped to hear him in any other way. If God is going to meet us, he must do so in the unique situation which defines our life. And so, if any of us meets God or notices his presence even in the shadows of daily life, then we have to conclude that there is something special about our particular situation.

If God speaks to me, or moves me, in the ordinary circumstances of my life—with my memories, my faults and virtues, likes and dislikes, given the people I live with and the characteristics of my body, then my place becomes special. It is special because it is specifically mine, because out of the materials of my life, God reveals himself to me. Because all the details of God's speaking or calling have to be tailored to fit my experience and background, how could

I not feel myself as especially noticed, selected, or chosen?

I should repeat the point: There is no other way for God to show himself to human beings apart from the concrete, everyday conditions and elements which pinpoint who I am and where I live. This holds as much for the Abrahams and St. Pauls of this world as it does for the millions of names and faces that are known only to God. To believe that God actually calls to us individually is to discover a new respect and reverence for the setting in which we have been placed.

Desire and call belong together. Our desires make it possible for us to hear a call, since God cannot call us to something we do not want. Sometimes, therefore, we find ourselves being awakened to desires that we did not realize were part of us. For unless we had desires—deep desires for life and peace—we could never be drawn toward God and we would never hear him no matter what address system he used. And unless some of our more particular desires had been shaped by the background experiences and situation from which we came, then we would not hear that particular word which God speaks to us personally; there would be no diversity of gifts and graces, no variety of ministries and service. In calling to us, therefore, God engages our deepest desires for life and peace as well as the particular ways of seeking life which mark and identify us. Desire becomes active under the force of a call; the calling that we hear discloses what we really want out of life.

Now, what does this have to do with traveling?

The urge to travel is another way of describing the call to journey, a call which the universe itself delivers to us. But the native restlessness of the human spirit is not a cosmic wanderlust. Restlessness refers to the inarticulate longing to be busy about our earthly pilgrimage, although none of us knows in advance what the contours of that journey may be, or what roads ought to be taken, or which set of directions need to be followed. In other words, by admitting that we are pilgrims and by wanting to be on our way, we open ourselves to God's call. And he calls each of us along that path which suits our longings and strengths. There is no one path for all, but there are an unlimited number of avenues, respecting the limitless ways in which human beings differ from one another.

Journeys give meaning and proportion to life. They impose purpose and direction upon experience. Knowing that we have a journey to make can help us to notice fresh colors in our life and to experience the uniqueness of the way which God wants to point out to us. Most of us, I think, look for some reassurance that life has a purpose, and the call to journey is an invitation to discover it. God alone reveals the purpose, and only God can issue the call. God is the master of journeys. When human experience cracks open under the pressure of restlessness and hope, the soul soon stirs with the force of its own mystery. Our situation starts to look special, our passage through this world becomes consequential. Someone wants us, calls us, chooses us, and directs us toward life.

One afternoon in Thailand, I was walking toward a small cottage. The path was interrupted by a 30-foot tree. Demons, I was informed later, only travel in straight lines. The tree had been planted in the middle of the path so that, as you curved around it, any stray demon on your trail would be prevented from following you indoors. People in Java have the custom of leaving a soft drink, or some rice and flowers, beneath a banyan tree for the spirits which inhabit its limbs. A single glance at a banyan tree would convince anyone that spirits are likely to dwell there. It looks like a walking forest.

We have no banyan trees in America, but ever since my acquaintance with Treebeard and the Entmoots in Tolkien's *Lord of the Rings,* my fondness for trees has grown considerably. What intrigues me about the Asian beliefs, however, is how nature ministers to a popular concern to keep spirits appeased and demons off our track by providing suitable habitats or appropriate defenses for our fears. The cry of the disciples sounds utterly human: "Who is this? Even the wind and the waves obey him!" (Mk 4:41). It is always possible to mistake God for a ghost when we are unfamiliar with his ways. What ghost in the sea had threatened the disciples that night?

I have referred several times to the human experience of being in transit in this world and, at the same time, of the urge to find our home, the center where we belong. The simplest way to resolve this paradox is to suggest that we always carry the center, the makings of our real security, inside us. It is from our hearts and out of our loves that we build our real homes. Yet that is only half right. Home is determined by what we love, not so much by the heart itself as by what the heart settles on. Since much of what the heart turns to may be inadequate, unsatisfying, perishable, or simply unworthy of our affection, we run the risk of bending the outgoing desires of the heart back upon itself and setting up our own selves as a true home, a secure place to dwell in.

This is the point at which ghosts come on the scene. The earth assumes a certain foreignness, even some hostility. Oceans and rivers, forests and mountains, night's shadows and the cavernous darkness between galaxies, dreams and memories too, become the forbidding abode or haunting signs of spirits and demons. Nature unlocks the closets which hide our deepest fears. And so we try to appease the hostile presence or flee to some haven where the demons will not find us. The earth refuses to let us feel at home until we learn the awesome dimensions of our inner space. What mighty tree shall we plant on the lane into our hearts to block the terrors and anxieties that stalk us from forcing their way inside? Homes cannot be built on the sand of our own selves.

Being-at-home happens when we love the right things. The same creatures which became the abode of ghosts when we turned fearful can show themselves as ministering spirits when our mind looks beyond itself. Sky and clouds, sea and mountains, noonday brightness and the silence of night, human beings and all their works of art, are passing through time. I shall exit from the universe long before the sun does, that star which lights and livens our world. But the sun is as much a creature as I am, and as creatures we share this mystery: Creatures point beyond themselves to something else as the source of their energy and life, their being and their destinies. Creatures are like pieces of music; they can be heard only when an orchestra plays them, and God is the orchestra. Without him the universe would fall utterly silent.

Journeying is a metaphor for life. It is an apt metaphor, since no one can step outside the movement of life except to die. Whether measured in years or in miles, the journey image suits us, for human beings are real travelers and not settlers or earthbound tourists. It may be, however, that the underside of human journeying is the God who makes a journey in us. God passes our way slowly, in strides which are more or less clearly defined, through that inner space which is our soul. Behind our dreams and fantasies, our wishes and fears, the decisions and planning of our daily living, it is often possible to detect another movement, to feel the pace or rhythm which is being set by the God who walks within us.

If we manage to turn our hearts toward loving what God loves, toward seeing what God sees, and toward imitating the way God behaves, then we shall understand in what sense the earth is not our home. The earth is the dwelling place of God. Even inside the chambers of our souls we may never feel entirely at home, for the soul too is the sanctuary and dwelling place of God. As the Psalmist wrote:

Lord, you have been our dwelling
      place
throughout all generations.
Before the mountains were born
or you brought forth the earth
      and the world,
from everlasting to everlasting
      you are God (Ps 90:1-2).

The traveler turns poor by laying aside the possessions that weigh him down, by taming the drive to acquire material things, by joining the procession of creatures as they pass through this world. But turning poor enters its critical phase as one starts to see the world as God sees it. Compassion lies at the root of religious vision, and this leads us into the next chapter.

# Interlude 4

The fourth beatitude recounted by Luke says: "Blessed are you when men hate you, when they exclude you and insult you and reject your name as evil, because of the Son of Man" (Lk 6:22). The qualifying phrase "because of the Son of Man" may be a clue about how we are supposed to hear the first three beatitudes, which could sound like this:

> Blessed are you who are poor, for Christ's sake.
> Blessed are you who hunger now, for the sake of
>     Christ.
> Blessed are you who weep now, for the sake of Christ.

This little change would help us to see that the disciples are the ones whom Jesus pronounces blessed. Their blessing consists in having been drawn into the life and experience of Jesus.

Jesus is the one who is poor, for our sake. Jesus is the one who suffers insult and rejection, hatred and persecution, for our sake. Jesus is the one who fasted in the desert and wept over the city of Jerusalem, for our sake. So, how does one become poor for Jesus' sake? Perhaps this can be answered by asking how that disciple is blessed who is called upon to suffer persecution for the sake of Jesus. After all, there is nothing holy about being persecuted or ridiculed; insult and injury are evils. Yet the fact that the disciple is in the position to share in Jesus' own experience, enduring the same things Jesus endured, is itself a grace. Paul thought so: "I want to know Christ," he wrote to the Philippians, "and the power of his resurrection and the fellowship of sharing in his sufferings, becoming like him in his death" (Ph 3:10).

So also, there is nothing holy about being hungry or poor. But if hunger and poverty are the result of one's companionship with Jesus, then one is indeed blessed.

When Jesus sent his disciples on their missionary journey—a journey they would undertake for his sake—he advised them to travel lightly and to stay mindful of their reason for being on the road. "Do not take along any gold or silver or copper in your belts; take no bag for the journey, or extra tunic, or sandals, or a staff" (Mt 10:9-10). Once in a village—they were not to go around sampling kitchens—they should stay in one house, "eating and drinking whatever they give you." They were not supposed to dally at street corners—"do not greet anyone on the road." The disciples might have identified themselves as missionaries, but perhaps Jesus was leading them to understand a further identity which they were adopting for his sake. To be a follower of Jesus meant taking up the way of a pilgrim.

"I am among you," Jesus said, "as one who serves" (Lk 22:27). One way in which Jesus served his disciples was to provide them an example they would always remember. They would return to that memory and perceive ever deeper meaning in what Jesus had done. At the time, the disciples would not have realized exactly how Jesus had served them, just as children usually don't realize the gift they have in the example of service which their parents set them until they become parents themselves.

Jesus tried to teach the disciples that the God whose Son they were following is above all a God who forgives. When words alone failed to persuade them about how serious Jesus was, he set them an example which they could never forget. God's compassion for men and women, and Jesus' certainty that God wanted men and women to believe in that compassion, were fused in the memory of the disciples by the sign of the cross. If in their own experience they could come to understand the compassion of God whose Son was hated, excluded, and insulted, then they would have won the greatest of blessings; grace would have triumphed in their hearts.

# 5

# The Forgiveness of Enemies and the Triumph of Grace

While they were stoning him, Stephen prayed, "Lord Jesus, receive my spirit." Then he fell on his knees and cried out, "Lord, do not hold this sin against them." When he had said this, he fell asleep.

Acts 7:59-60

Much has been said in the last few chapters about journeying and being poor. Most of those who read these pages have had experiences of "existential poverty," that is, the native poverty of the human condition. They will not have shared in the poverty which spells nakedness, hunger, malnutrition, overcrowded hospitals, and scratching the earth in the scorching sun. But I don't think that one has to undergo such experiences in order to appreciate what it means to be poor. There is nothing glamorous about destitution. Material poverty can give birth to courage, determination, and even nobility of soul. But it just as easily breeds political paralysis, greed, and despair; it gives rise to violence, revolution, and war. Remove material poverty by feeding, clothing, educating, employing, and housing people in ways that befit human dignity, and you remove the exasperation on which violence thrives. But existential poverty will remain. It may lie hidden under the spoils of economic well-being, but unless it is acknowledged and understood, existential poverty can bankrupt societies and nations, even entire civilizations.

This chapter introduces the prayer which poor men and women might feel drawn to make. Again, for most of those who read these pages the forgiveness of enemies will probably be a notional or spiritually harmless concern. While there may be many people whom we dislike or who do not get along with us, we do not live with the chilling effect of having real enemies. Of course, there are the Russians. I grew up with the conviction that Russia was God's chief enemy. During grammar school, the air-raid drills and civil-defense posters awakened the fear of death in me, and we prayed the rosary fervently for the conversion of Russia. Today, though I prefer not to believe that a whole nation would want another world war, I do believe that another country might be as afraid of us as we have been of them. But my contact with Russia has been indirect. I have read and heard about Russia's weapons and ways, I know that we are trying to arm as many nations as possible against them, and I know that Russia's leaders have little respect for personal freedom. Are the Russians my enemies, people on whom I have never laid eyes?

No one has ever defrauded me of land, pillaged my crops, threatened my children, murdered my neighbors, damaged my reputation, interrogated me under torture, barred me from church, censored my books, or refused me my wages. I have not been bullied by the police, and I do not live in a village which has been tormented by guerillas. But these things happen. Perhaps then I do not have real enemies. To pray for their forgiveness is unnecessary; at least it requires no effort. I am perplexed by the many psalms which hound God for justice and complain bitterly about powerful enemies because these prayers do not relate to my part of the world.

But we do not have to have enemies in order to experience the competing powers of love and hate within our souls. A passage from Alan Paton's *Cry, the Beloved Country* observed:

> Some of us think when we have power, we shall revenge ourselves on the white man who has had

power, and because our desire is corrupt, we are cor-
rupted, and the power has no heart in it. But most
white men do not know this truth about power, and
they are afraid lest we get it.

All of us are capable of vengeance. And when the thirst for
revenge whets our appetite for power, we cannot recognize
other men and women as fellow sojourners on the earth;
they take on the annoying, maddening, fearsome features of
enemies who must be subdued. Perhaps, then, the crucial
issue is not whether we can identify who our real and imagined enemies are, but whether we shall ever be able to look
at the world in such a way that no one could be our enemy:
not that we could never again be victimized, but that as far
as we are concerned, the very possibility of distinguishing
between friends and enemies vanishes. In the end, there
would only be sisters and brothers.

The fifth-century monastic writer, John Cassian, once
wrote:

> No matter what provokes it, anger blinds the soul's
> eyes, preventing it from seeing the Sun of
> righteousness. Leaves, whether of gold or lead, placed
> over the eyes, obstruct the sight equally, for the value
> of the gold does not affect the blindness it produces.
> Similarly, anger, whether reasonable or unreasonable,
> obstructs our spiritual vision.

The same rule, it seems to me, should apply to God. Anger
would block his vision as much as it would blind ours. And
whatever ensures the clarity of God's vision must be the in-
gredient that would safeguard the quality of ours.

Because the Father is a God of forgiveness, Jesus instructed his disciples to pray, "Forgive us our sins, for we
also forgive everyone who sins against us" (Lk 11:4). Reconciliation and forgiveness improve our spiritual vision so that
we can stand in the divine presence:

"Therefore, if you are offering your gift at the altar
and there remember that your brother has something
against you, leave your gift there in front of the altar.
First go and be reconciled to your brother; then come
and offer your gift" (Mt 5:23-24).

God's vision is always clear because he sees the world with
compassionate and forgiving eyes. Jesus calls us to the same
way of viewing things, but between his call and its realization in our lives there must come the redemption of our inner vision. To forgive those whom we love is not always
easy; to forgive our enemies may prove very bitter. Such
forgiveness, even for God, exacts the highest price. The sign
of the crucified Jesus should prevent us from forgetting that
God was not blinded by anger when, in Jesus, he experienced the reality of evil; neither must anger ever be allowed
to blind us.

Prayer for the forgiveness of one's enemies bears the
gospel hallmark as no other prayer does. Jesus' summons to
that kind of prayer marks the central Christian word:

"But I tell you, Love your enemies and pray for those
who persecute you, that you may be sons of your
Father in heaven" (Mt 5:44-45).

This is the word which Jesus fully incarnated at the moment
of his death:

"Father, forgive them, for they do not know what they
are doing" (Lk 23:34).

In that prayer, Jesus proved himself to be the Son.

But what are we asking of God in making the prayer for
the forgiveness of enemies, and why should making that
prayer be so difficult? A moment's review of the terrible
evils which have been inflicted upon so many people by
other human beings should make it obvious why the words
begging God to forgive one's enemies might refuse to leave

one's lips. Our sense of justice demands sanctions against the gangsters and terrorists of history, and yet the prayer for forgiveness is imploring God to pardon them. Supposing that the prayer on behalf of our enemies is heard, does this mean that God has acceded to our request and that our enemies get away scot-free?

This question, I believe, brings to the surface of our spiritual experience one of the most critical and potentially threatening insights into the Christian relationship with God. It would be simple to argue that forgiveness depends upon repentance, that the route to repentance is often the path of wisdom gained through suffering, that God sends or permits suffering for the sake of conversion, and that the prayer for forgiveness implicitly asks God for all of this.

But I wonder. Doesn't the prayer on behalf of enemies, as we intend it, unfold in a less complicated way? That prayer, like the prayer of Jesus from the cross and like the prayer of Stephen in clear imitation of Jesus, only asks that the Father should forgive men and women who harm us because they do not know what they have done. What then would it mean if God should hear and answer this prayer? We need to explore this question in some detail.

## The Significance of the Prayer

Clearly, we should not interpret Jesus' prayer for his persecutors to mean that he was trying to turn the Father from his anger. God's attitude toward human beings was already one of reconciling love. The words of Jesus reflect the congruence of his own spiritual vision—his compassion and love—with the Father's desire to heal the world. God's regard for the human race remains steadfast and loving both before and after the crucifixion, otherwise it would be impossible to explain why he sent his Son to live among us. God is always merciful. The prayer we make for the forgiveness of those who have wronged us, like the prayer of Jesus, does not persuade God to change his attitude from hostility to compassion. God is compassionate by nature, and this accounts for his creating the world and revealing himself. To speculate for a moment, even if there are other planets and other histories where God has creatures for whom he cares, is it not unreasonable to think that God would have created a world where his saving love would not be victorious? We should not separate God's creative work from his compassion, his love, and his determination to share himself. No planet, no place in the universe where free creatures struggle under the mystery of sin and grace, should be allowed to fail. Would it be presumptuous to conclude that God could not create a world in which the majority of his creatures would never achieve their destined union with him?

The question needs to be phrased this way in order to avoid the unsettling notion that God might not love some people enough in order for them to reach salvation. When, in the 16th century, St. Robert Bellarmine was commenting on Jesus' prayer from the cross, he noted that Jesus' prayer was not universally victorious because the grace of conversion had been granted only to those who were ordained to everlasting life (see Acts 13:48). Forgiveness, after all, is contingent upon repentance. Since not everyone at the scene of the crucifixion had repented, not everyone had been forgiven. But, one might ask, why would God deprive some people of the grace of repentance?

The problem is intractable. It creates all sorts of technical difficulties about the relation between grace and free will, and it erodes the Christian understanding of why God created human beings—not just some but all of us—in the first place.

The problem continues to be stubborn even when looked at through the 13th-century theological perspective of Thomas Aquinas. In the questions of his *Summa Theologica* which deal with prayer, St. Thomas inquired whether we ought to pray for our enemies. First of all

Thomas argued, the Bible frequently inveighs against the enemies of ancient Israel (who were also enemies of God), and the Bible is God's revealed word. Secondly, if Christian nations were obliged to pray for their enemies, then something close to spiritual schizophrenia would result. How could a nation engage in war if it must pray for its enemies while at the same time it was fighting to conquer them? Following Augustine's lead, Thomas pointed out that we can hate the sin and love the sinner. Thus we are free to beg God to correct evildoers for their own eternal good. Prayer of this kind is not directed against sinful men and women but against the reign of sin, which is the cause of our having enemies in the first place.

Thomas went on to say that we have to respect the divine will to condemn those who persevere in their sin. But because temporal evils might hasten them to reform, we can legitimately pray that our enemies suffer misfortune. We can even attack them so as to restrain them from sin. To pray for our enemies is a matter of charity. To love them, however, is a matter of perfection, and perfection can be urged but not commanded. The love of enemies demands asceticism. From the sinner's side, there will be no forgiveness without repentance. In his *Catena Aurea*, Thomas cited a remark from Bede, who was commenting on Luke 17:3-4. The scriptural text reads:

> "If your brother sins, rebuke him, and if he repents, forgive him. If he sins against you seven times in a day, and seven times comes back to you and says, 'I repent,' forgive him."

"But we must mark," said Bede in the citation by St. Thomas, "that he does not forgive everyone who sins, but him only who repents of his sins." Thus the integrity of divine justice is upheld.

Bede was writing in the early part of the eighth century, and his comment on Luke 23:34 may be a bit more interesting. The fact that some people went away from Calvary beating their breasts indicates that they had received the grace of conversion and, therefore, that Jesus' prayer for their forgiveness must have been answered on the spot:

> For one must not think that he prayed the Father for these things in vain, but that undoubtedly he implored on behalf of those who came to believe after his passion because he had been praying for them.

Other people left the scene still hating Jesus, which would lead us to conclude that Jesus must not have prayed for them:

> Certainly, it should be noted that he did not offer prayers to the Father for those who were inflamed with envy and pride, and preferred to crucify rather than confess the one whom they understood to be the Son of God. He prayed particularly for those who were zealous for God but not according to knowledge, and did not know what they had done.

Bede then recalls a verse from the First Letter of John: "There is a sin that leads to death. I am not saying that he should pray about that" (1 Jn 5:16). The meaning of this verse is by no means clear, although Bede apparently took it to mean that there are some sinners for whom we need not pray. He concludes his comment, however, with a slightly different note:

> Imitate your Lord, therefore, and intercede for your enemies. And if you are not yet able to do this, at least beware of presuming to pray against them. For thus having made progress day by day you will reach the point when you too will be able to pray on their behalf.

A text which throws better light on the prayer for the

forgiveness of enemies comes in the fourth century from St. John Chrysostom's Eighteenth Homily on the Gospel of Matthew. Chrysostom was no stranger to persecution, and he understood the call to imitate divine perfection. He saw that love of enemies proves that we are the Father's true daughters and sons. Jesus had set the measure of how far we must strive in order to imitate God.

In the first place, Chrysostom reminds his audience, no one suffered from his enemies so much as Christ did. Secondly, the anger and hatred afflicting our enemies is a far graver disease than the evil we suffer, and our endurance might provide the healing example which will cure them of their sickness. But in the third place, there is the divine example itself. Chrysostom wrote:

> Having seen God become man for your sake, do you still inquire and doubt how it is possible to forgive your fellow servants their injuries against you? Do you not hear him on the cross saying, "Forgive them, for they do not know what they are doing"?

In his compassion, Jesus perfectly imitated the Father's love. The prayer for the forgiveness of enemies is, therefore, the highest expression of being like God. Because of the love from which this prayer comes, it is also the chief sign of Christian perfection. Jesus on the cross dramatically restated what he had taught in the Sermon on the Mount.

Let us return to the speculative question raised earlier about whether God could have created a world where most of his creatures failed to arrive at salvation. The question is of interest, not because it can be answered, but because it forces us to reflect on our experience of God. What kind of God do Christians encounter? There is a healthy strain of theological optimism riding through contemporary theology. This hopefulness did not arise because theologians uncovered fresh data on God; it arose from a confident appraisal of Christian experience. Christian belief in the sovereignty of *grace* commits us to acknowledging the utter graciousness of our eventual union with God. The very possibility of union with God—our being called into existence, our capacity for laughter and love, our desire for life and peace—is also sheer grace. But our belief also requires us to notice that God's graciousness is primarily expressed in his loving and free decision to create the world. But a world in which large numbers of creatures failed to reach their creative purpose would throw into doubt the *sovereignty* of grace.

This conviction controlled the theological perspective of Origen, the great Christian thinker of the third century. Given the hold that sin has on some people, Origen argued, the patient grace of God will have to continue to touch and transform them even beyond their existence on earth. Having made us for himself, it is unthinkable that the divine plan should remain eternally unfulfilled even in the case of a single creature. Writing in the third book of his work *On First Principles*, Origen said:

> For God deals with souls not in view of the short time of our life here, which is confined to some 60 or a few more years, but in view of the everlasting and eternal age, exercising his providential care over souls that are immortal, just as he himself is eternal and immortal. For he made our rational nature, which he created "in his own image and likeness," incorruptible, and therefore the soul, which is immortal, is not shut out by the shortness of our present life from the divine healing and remedies.

With a bold stroke, Origen went on to conclude that just because the Pharaoh had drowned in the sea, we should not suppose that God's providential designs on his behalf had come to an end! God cared for the Pharaoh too.

Origen's views eventually got him into trouble, although this is not the place to explain why. But can the conviction about the final triumph of grace be rescued without subscribing to Origen's theory that the process of purification and instruction persists beyond this life? The answer may be tied up with the prayer for the forgiveness of enemies. Our theological tradition has insisted that the divine will is immutable, but this is not the static immutability of an unfeeling creator. What remains unchanging in God is the steadiness of his compassion and love, his readiness to accept and forgive. This is the way God was before Adam sinned; it is the way we encounter him now.

The prayer of Jesus on the cross—"Father, forgive them"—distills the essence of Christian discipleship. God loves the world, sinners and saints alike. Human beings exist because God loves, and so God sees all of his creatures as people whom he loves. God urges us to love our enemies, but clearly God himself has none. In his vision of us, no one is a stranger; no one is unloved. This is the perspective that God wants us to share; it is this inner vision which is revealed so strikingly in the prayer of the crucified Jesus.

## The Salvation of the Many and the Holiness of a Few

No one will quarrel with the proposition that God not only created the world, but he still is creating the world, which is another way of stating that he is even now saving or redeeming it. But it is important to notice that God creates and saves *the world*. Certainly, God forms us as individuals and he meets each of us personally. But if we step back and ask about what exactly God is doing by creating and redeeming each of us, then our attention shifts to a wider arena of grace. God is fashioning the human race, with its diversity of cultures and languages, its individual people and nations, into the people of God. The church, we believe, is a sign of God's intention. Many people, however, conceive salvation too narrowly. They do not think of salvation beyond the limits of each individual life, beginning with their own. This view is incomplete.

The grace of God is personal, but it is never private. Whatever God gives to any one of us eventually works its way into the lives of others. Just as the sin of one person or one group, like a stone thrown into a pond, ripples in ever wider circles, so too the virtue of one spreads out to inspire or to challenge other people and groups. The human story has been shaped by our solidarity in Adam's sin, but surely our fortunes have been no less affected by our solidarity in the obedience of Christ. St. Paul wrote: "For as in Adam all die, so in Christ all will be made alive" (1 Cor 15:22).

Abraham had secured God's promise that Sodom would be spared for the sake of ten righteous people (Gn 18:32). How much more should God be willing to spare the human race for the sake of the one in whom he was so well pleased! (Mk 1:11). The prayer which Jesus spoke when he reached his final hour—the hour when he drew all things to himself (Jn 12:32)—that prayer spoken from the cross when he appeared as the great high priest (Heb 7:26-27), is the most dramatic example of a priestly prayer. It is a prayer on behalf of others. Those who find themselves lured by the naked grace of that sign—Jesus praying for his enemies from the cross—are being attracted, it seems to me, toward living as a priestly people (1 Pt 2:9). They will discover their deepest experience of God when they are enabled to make the same prayer which Jesus made.

The priestly nature of the prayer for the forgiveness of enemies cannot be understood apart from a profound spiritual response in the face of unjust suffering, a response formed in the soul's vision of how God himself compassionately holds and loves the world. That prayer is priestly, not because we are interceding with an offended God on behalf of others, but because it carries into the world Jesus' own experience of God. The words of Luke 23:34 remind us that Jesus on the cross rendered the Father's love personally and really present to human history. In the same way, those who follow Jesus show their priesthood when their living and their compassion allow the God of Jesus Christ to be really and personally present in the world. Would it be too much to suggest that the salvation of the human race may depend on the holiness of those—however many or however few—who have surrendered to the powerful example of Jesus? Perhaps all people will be saved because of the solidarity we enjoy with the saints who have appeared in human history. And chief among those holy ones is Jesus himself.

The prayer for the forgiveness of enemies represents a triumph of divine grace working in and through human nature, fashioning the soul so that it feels toward the world as God himself does. In Jesus, grace worked so well that the divine and human perfectly united. His words and actions, his death and resurrection, bear witness to the triumph of grace. Jesus was as much truly God as he was truly one of us. That same grace moves within Jesus' disciples, helping them to be the enduring sign that God's love has been and is now stronger than the power of hate.

Now how does this affect our idea of salvation?

Surely, salvation encompasses more than the individual's achievement of eternal life. Salvation cannot be compared to passing a test, for one takes a test alone. In our world the Spirit is acting to gather people into communion, as Vatican II said, and there is no room for purely private graces. How can we consider our personal salvation without thinking of those who are close to us? Just as we choose sides in a game and identify with a team in its wins and losses, so also we shall win or lose salvation together. Salvation involves communities, weaving its way through all the generations of human history. With life-giving breath the Spirit fashions people in every age who will reflect the loving kindness of God. Because we are tied to the fortunes of our planet by decisions and events over which we have little or no control, we are dragged into a sinfulness which webs through the entire social fabric and finds its way into our own families and into the remote corners of our soul. "But where sin increased," St. Paul wrote, "grace increased all the more" (Rom 5:20). Solidarity in evil should be matched by solidarity in goodness, if one takes seriously the corporate nature of human existence. Everyone is invited to contribute to the ultimate success of God's creative aims for our planet, but the successful outcome of our endeavors may carry along even those who consciously or unconsciously worked against us.

Does the intuition which I am trying to articulate sound extravagant? Perhaps it is. But after all, we already believe that many people have been saved without personal effort, such as infants and innocent children who die, or those who are mentally handicapped. Can God afford this extravagance? These are not exceptional cases of divine grace. Certainly this is less extravagant than what we read in the gospel concerning the great banquet:

> "Go out quickly into the streets and alleys of the town and bring in the poor, the crippled, the blind and the lame" (Lk 14:21).

Divine love does not intend to save only an elected few, including by way of exception those who were deprived of the possibility of exercising free choice, and those who were so destitute that they were unable to think of the things of God. Salvation should not be reckoned so tightly in terms of individual accomplishments and exceptional cases. The gospels portray a God who is consistently overgenerous with his forgiveness and grace.

A successful outcome of the human story need not require that the largest number of people should become perfect; it does demand that there should be at least some who have demonstrated the human soul's capacity for great love. History will have proven successful and worthy of the divine effort if there are in every age people who realized human nature's openness to divine grace and its ability to

118

triumph over resentment, injustice, and violence. They show this by their readiness to forgive their enemies, to pray for them, and even to love them. The presence of these disciples of Jesus throughout history testifies to humanity's soundest achievement. For all eternity they will enjoy knowing that they furthered God's creative plan. Their sisters and brothers will realize that although they did not promote God's designs, they were unable to impede the eventual triumph of grace. Theirs will be the humble joy of realizing that they had been carried into glory by the love of those whom they had persecuted. And why not? This is exactly what the saints prayed that God would do! It pleased God to create a world in which the prayer for the forgiveness of enemies would be made.

If it should prove to be the case (we shall not know for certain until eternity dawns) that the majority of people are saved through the perseverance of a few, then I am still at a loss to explain why God arranged things this way. But neither can anyone explain why the grace of repentance should bear fruit in some but not in others. There is always the danger of trying to locate reasons which God never revealed, and there is the danger of being scandalized by divine generosity.

"Lord," Stephen asked, "do not hold this sin against them." And we have been looking at the intention behind this prayer. The conviction that salvation is not a private victory of the individual but always relates in some measure to the whole human story strikes me as particularly Catholic. Looked at from another side, if some people were to lose their souls, then their tragedy would not be a purely private affair either. Their loss would remain an everlasting reminder of that portion of the human adventure which failed. They would become the human residue of those who refused to cooperate with God's creative pull upon the world, the ones who despoiled history and chose to have no part in the lasting human enterprise, the ones who reaped everlasting isolation. Whether or not any human being can renounce his or her membership in human history by withdrawing from our solidarity in sin and in grace seems to me to be an open question. History cannot be reduced to an arena where individual players act out solo performances in which they win or lose eternal life by themselves alone.

One further point ought to be made. As long as there is life on the earth, human beings will maintain their concern in the outcome of history. Jesus did not ascend to God's right hand, as we profess, in order to wait passively while his disciples carried out their mission. Jesus is alive and active among us through his Spirit, drawing and encouraging us to live out the gospel. So also the saints have not transcended their concern for what happens on the earth once they reached God's presence. Rather, they perceive the mystery of salvation yet unfolding on the earth from the inner side of grace. Unless we believed them to stay concerned about us, it would make no sense to ask their intercession. And if the drama of salvation does have dimensions elsewhere in the universe, the concern of the saints will extend to histories besides our own. It takes no leap of imagination, however, to see that the satisfaction which we shall enjoy for eternity can never be dissociated from the overall success of human history and from our knowledge that we contributed in some small way to the kingdom of justice, love, and peace. If any of us wins salvation without having added anything of value to the human story, it will be on account of the compassion and loving kindness of those who prayed on our behalf.

## Conclusion

I have used the phrase "successful history" rather freely and loosely, so by way of conclusion several comments may be in order.

First, the final judgment about what is successful belongs to God. He made the world and he alone can determine whether his designs have been fulfilled. Is a history in which the Son of God was crucified successful? What about a history in which righteous people are raised from the dead? Was the Incarnation an afterthought, or did God hope that Adam would never sin? How reasonable do we think that God's expectations of us really are? Christ would not have come if there were no sin in the world, but sin is an inevitable feature of a world where free creatures are in the process of coming to know and accept God's love. So it seems to me.

The only standard of success, then, is the degree to which humanity has been touched and transformed by the Spirit, and only God perceives the depth of that change. I have proposed that the prayer for the forgiveness of enemies indicates a soul grasped by the Spirit. Compassion is the mark of perfection because God himself is forgiving and compassionate. This we are certain of, because the true icon of God's love was revealed to us in the Jesus who prayed, "Father, forgive them." Perhaps the success of the human effort will not consist of the largest number of people becoming holy, but of a small number, truly of God, who appear consistently throughout history. By the intensity of their love, the universality of their compassion, and their dependence on God's grace, these people of God actualize in every generation humanity's solidarity in the mystery of goodness. Because of them the rest of us draw hope that all of humanity will be saved. The many will be carried along by the holiness of priestly people.

Second, the reader may be wondering uncomfortably why anyone would struggle to do good if the prospect of salvation looks assured, thanks to the prayers of the saints. But a minute's pause should be enough to notice where this difficulty comes from. The generosity of God can be disturbing, especially when our motives are mixed between the love of God and the fear of hell. The idea of reward without work might put a thorn in our dedication to the gospel. However, those who truly know God are less likely to ask why they should be laboring for the kingdom while others stand all day idle. Those who know God continue to seek his presence because that is the way they are. They want life and they have found the fullness of life is God himself. They do not worry about defending a strict merit system for salvation, for mercy is of greater concern to them than justice. This attitude arises from their familiarity with God. The rest of us may ask why we should bother to live uprightly if God is going to be so generous, but not those who have found God. Only when inner vision is blocked by resentment, outrage, anger, or envy, do we find ourselves threatened by God's love; we may then abandon the sign of the cross. The last prayer of Jesus is a testament from one who knew what God is like.

There is no way to explain why people seek God, why they feel drawn to love God and their neighbors, or why they are willing to undergo purification of soul in the darkness and confusion of their sinfulness. But in their experience of God they are moved to ask him to grant eternal life to others, even to those at whose hands they endured rejection, ridicule, and death. There is no way of accounting for this, unless human nature has been so created that it will always be haunted by the Spirit's call. We are not made for ourselves but for the God who lives; this fact cannot be escaped. Only this explains why some people move beyond religious indifference, beyond fear of punishment, beyond a need to see sanctions, to discover the God of our Lord Jesus Christ.

### A Difficulty and an Answer

The reader may want to remind me of a gospel text that presents another word about divine forgiveness, a word which is perhaps a bit more realistic:

"For if you forgive men when they sin against you, your heavenly Father will also forgive you. But if you do not forgive men their sins, your Father will not forgive your sins" (Mt 6:14-15).

Doesn't Jesus imply that God's forgiveness is contingent upon our readiness to forgive others? Maybe he does, but we ought to ask who those "others" might be. "If you do not forgive men their sins": Is Jesus referring to our brothers and sisters, or to our friends and neighbors—the ones whom we should be prepared to forgive not just seven times, but seventy times seven times (Mt 18:22)? Or could Jesus mean that we must be ready to forgive all, even our enemies, if we expect God to forgive us? And if this is the case, will God delay his forgiveness until our love has become so perfect that it embraces our enemies? In short, this text may be challenging us again with the highest of Christian ideals.

Jesus devoted much of his ministry to helping sinners to repent. One might wonder, along with people like Bede and Bellarmine, what makes repentance so urgent if divine forgiveness can be obtained even without our repenting. I would suggest that Jesus' ministry consisted primarily of telling people that they belonged to God. Jesus managed to persuade his disciples of the Father's love, and he enabled them to begin an entirely new chapter in their relationship with God. Repentance was the gospel's code word for change of heart, for turning toward God and discovering his concerns. Unless repentance grew out of an encounter with the kindness and grace so tangible in the words and works of Jesus, then Jesus would have achieved little else than to stir people's awareness of why they should feel guilty in God's presence. Of course, human beings often have plenty to feel guilty about, but Jesus would be no savior if he left matters there. For, finally, what matters is God himself, the one who keeps challenging our minds and hearts to hear what is true and worthwhile, the one who refuses to leave us alone. Guilt and fear might prompt repentance, but we have to grow beyond the stage of being fearful of God or feeling guilty over our past life. Even Jesus could not speak about fearing God without immediately adding a word about not being afraid:

> "I tell you, my friends, do not be afraid of those who kill the body and after that can do no more. But I will show you whom you should fear: Fear him who, after killing the body, has power to throw you into hell. Yes, I tell you, fear him" (Lk 12:4-5).

But then Jesus follows this warning with the words:

> "Are not five sparrows sold for two pennies? Yet not one of them is forgotten by God. Indeed, the very hairs of your head are all numbered. Don't be afraid; you are worth more than many sparrows" (12:6-7).

Our hesitation over assenting to a generous view of divine forgiveness stems, I think, from our inability to reconcile God's mercy with God's justice. Yet, justice and mercy are not two sides of God's attitude toward the world; they are two poles within our religious experience. The human condition, which characterizes every one of us, shows itself as both sinful and graced. As our relationship with God develops, we can become afraid: We become increasingly conscious of our inadequacy and sin, we start to remember biblical passages about the punishments which God visits upon sinners, we doubt our worthiness of any divine favor, and we dare not presume upon God's mercy. But part of our failing is that we do not trust God's love and do not fully believe in his compassion. Such is the tension of truth within which spiritual creatures live: We know our inner poverty and we experience ourselves as loved by God. On the one hand, the presumptive soul runs away from its inner poverty by ignoring its utter dependence on God's mercy and love. The timid soul, on the other hand, does not yet believe that the loving kindness of God is everlasting. Our failing to forgive one another, even our enemies, measures how much we have presumed upon God's kindness by not grasping the dimensions of our own inner need of grace.

To suggest that there is ever a time when God is not forgiving would both diminish and defeat the initiatives of grace. Our reluctance to forgive one another prevents us from sharing in the freedom with which God loves the world, but that failure does not alter God's desire to approach us. The text in which Jesus speaks of God's not forgiving us unless we pardon one another describes, I hope, a moment within our religious experience. How can we expect the Lord to do for us what we are not ready to do for one another? But then again, we must hope that God will do for us what we have not done for each other precisely because we are as yet incapable of greatness, and because God's heart and will are much larger than ours. Maybe this is not the soundest interpretation of Jesus' words, but I don't see the harm in attempting to hear Jesus speak to us from within the ideal of the divine-human relationship which he enjoyed and to which he draws his disciples.

When our spiritual journey begins in a confrontation with personal sin (as is so often the case), it is hard to avoid thinking about the claims of divine justice. Our apprehension over that justice forces us to wait upon God's mercy. But sometimes the spiritual journey opens on a different path. God looks upon us with love, and the first spiritual moment can be an experience of God's kindness. Only in a second or third moment does consciousness of sin cause us to wonder how we could be worthy of divine love; we are stunned into a different experience of divine justice. God's justice manifests itself in his faithfulness to creation, as Paul insisted in his Letter to the Romans. Divine forgiveness does not depend upon our repentance, or on our ability to love our enemies, or our doing heroic, virtuous deeds. God's forgiveness depends only on the love out of which he fashioned the human race. Christ is God's pledge that having loved the world, he will be faithful and forgiving to the end.

# 6
## Some Notes on Being Religious

And the Lord said, "I will cause all my goodness to pass in front of you, and I will proclaim my name, the Lord, in your presence. I will have mercy on whom I will have mercy, and I will have compassion on whom I will have compassion. But," he said, "you cannot see my face, for no one may see me and live." Then the Lord said, "There is a place near me where you may stand on a rock. When my glory passes by, I will put you in a cleft in the rock and cover you with my right hand until I have passed by. Then I will remove my hand and you will see my back; but my face must not be seen."

Exodus 33:19-23

The road to Godavari (where I am now sitting) first heads straight, cutting through the rich, almost breathable greens of rice and maize; but then it is forced to bend around one of the tiny settlements along the sloping and winding few miles out of Kathmandu valley into the southeastern hills. Although Godavari sits no more than 500 feet above the floor of the valley, the climb takes you out of the hot and usually congested air of the city. Ahead of you stands Pholchowki, which rises some 9,000 feet and is the highest point of the broad hills stretching around Kathmandu. From Godavari you can watch the morning haze lift from the valley below. When the clouds in the northwestern sky clear away, Godavari commands an enviable view of the Himalayan peaks—Ganesh Himal, Himalchuli (which towers over 25,000 feet), and Manaslu (the world's eighth highest mountain). Even from 40 or 50 miles away, the

127

glaciers turning orange under the morning sun must be one of our planet's most ruggedly beautiful pictures.

It was early October. The last storm of the monsoon season, one of the worst in several decades, emptied the water it had carried up from the Bay of Bengal, and the downpour so gouged the deforested slopes that the rivers rushed a little more of Nepal back to the bay. Swollen creeks lying in the wrinkles of the hills turned into torrents. Brick-and-clay homes, so conveniently built by the banks of a friendly stream, crumbled apart. Goats and chickens belonging to many a poor family, fields of ripe corn and rice, dozens of villagers too, were caught by the force of the rapids and washed away. In nine hours, ten inches of rain had fallen.

The Godavari bridge was another casualty of the storm. This meant that to go to town you had to cross the creek over a hastily erected footbridge consisting of a few pieces of roofing metal lying across two narrow iron rails, which were pinned to the banks with large rocks. From there you walk the dirt path around the corner of a marble quarry and join the people on the far side of the broken bridge who are waiting to board the blue bus. Village people in Third-World countries age quickly, and even the buses, after only two months of service on the Godavari road, were already showing the strain of working for the poor.

On they come: men, women, children. They flag down the bus, a few people from one village, several more from another, while standing along the brief stretches of open road or in front of small, damp cottages with cracked mud walls and straw roofs. They pile into the seats and cram the aisle, and even cling to the side with just a toehold on the landing step. The doorways look like beehives. Next to me sat a man with two roosters, a large burlap sack of rice, and three of the longest radishes I ever saw. Outside, the early morning passed us by: women washing clothes and boys scrubbing water buffalos in one of the shallow cisterns or mud holes that collect ground water, red peppers strung from shutters and doorways to dry in the sun, chickens darting away from the bus tires, a few old people squatting on mats and looking after the children who were sailing leaves in the water which ran from the sewers and drains, goats nibbling at the leafy shrubs dotting the small patches of standing rice.

With October comes the holiday season for Hindu and Buddhist alike. Inside the bus, memories of the flood had temporarily faded. People chattered excitedly, their minds now turned to the business which was bringing them to the valley. What, I was imagining, would the kingdom of God be like? Would God pack us into his kingdom like crates of chickens being trucked into glory? The image was both amusing and engaging. The bus ride had plunged me into the middle of an everyday world where life rubbed on all sides with its brightness, its dependence on the earth, its cries and smells and smiles, its coughing and spitting, its sudden tragedy, uncomplicated concerns, and intense natural beauty. And the bus was no place for keeping secrets. From the smell of your breath to the grease on your clothes or the wart on your neck or the business of the day. "Relax," some inner voice was urging. "Laugh a little, because you belong to this mixture of soil and flesh, of tears and breath, of laughter and love too." That was a warming voice.

For as long as I can recall, I've puzzled over the possible ways of piecing together my relationship to people whose lives had been unfolding beyond my own family and neighborhood, beyond my home town and country, even beyond my own culture and history. For all eternity we shall be more closely united with people who are now strangers to us than we are joined here to our brothers and sisters, our friends and lovers, our parents and children. Picture them as they assemble: women and men, from every land and culture since the days of Adam and Eve; those born into destitution and those born into riches, every Dives of the earth and every Lazarus that prayed him into heaven; doctors, soldiers, children, princes, thieves and saints, millions upon millions of them, those once healthy or insane or diseased. We shall be drawn into the deepest secrets of all these people—and they will peer into ours—not out of some final satisfaction to human curiosity but in the experience of knowing and being known. For the mystery of grace will unravel and display the secret which each human being is, the intricate way in which the finger of God has fashioned us. There will be no blushing as our inner self unfolds for all eyes to see, only the hush of wonder. Who does not want to be in the company of people he loves, people who care for her? And is it not true that we grow in our affection for others as we come to know them better? Loving makes it possible to know another person. But there is also real pleasure in being known, in realizing that someone else knows and understands us to the bottom of our souls, or at least as far down as we let them look.

Perhaps only God will ever know us to the very bottom, where our spirit leaves off and God's Spirit begins. But still, where would we be without friends and loved ones to understand us? In God's kingdom, I would imagine, all secrets would disappear in the knowing which comes from great friendship. "I have called you friends," Jesus said, "for everything that I learned from my Father I have made known to you."

Human beings share a common destiny; we have to go where the planet goes. That much is a truism. But we also have to pass under the eye of God; and when he sees us, God does not find strangers, only friends. To be able to see the world with the eye of God! What joins human beings together is so much deeper (though not always more powerful) than what divides us. Most men and women, as they advance in years, stay interested in the lives of their children and, particularly, of their grandchildren. Couldn't we suppose that in God's kingdom we shall awaken to an interest in the life of the human race from one generation to the next? Perhaps we shall even be able to follow with delight the ongoing construction of the universe and the creation of new life. Who can say? But unless eternity turns into an everlasting nap—which I hope never happens—something will have to keep us alert and concerned. We may be required to surrender our personal consciousness in order to learn how to be conscious together, in that dimension of love and peace which unites Christ to the Father. Again, who can say? Somehow we shall be drawn into one another through our union with God. We shall have to part with our privacy, our secrets, and our wariness of strangers. A bus ride every now and then may help in getting accustomed to the idea.

Asia refreshes my religious sense in still another way. To live for a while in the middle of religious practices, symbols, and ideas which are not Christian is both humbling and liberating. You learn the unforgettable lesson that Christianity does not lie at the center of religion; God does. Jesus must have startled his disciples when he responded to their fascination with the splendor of the temple buildings by forecasting destruction: "I tell you the truth, not one stone here will be left on another; every one will be thrown down" (Mt 24:2). The legacy of faith which is the word of God, not buildings, is the only monument that survives. Asia seems to say that there is no religious monopoly on God's grace, and that divinity does not attach itself to customs, buildings, institutions, or doctrines. Divinity comes to human beings as they become people of God.

But more concretely, many of my Western church concerns appear less important in the Far East. Ecclesiastical issues about authority, the ordination of women, clerical celibacy, and so on, as well as theological doctrine about the divinity of Christ, papal infallibility, the virgin birth, and so on, are relativized by the enormous pressures of hunger, ignorance, and the thirst for justice and political voice. The most persistent threats to world peace are hunger and economic insecurity, and the political instability which proceeds from these two evils. The scourges of hunger, injustice, and political repression challenge the relevance of every religious doctrine (Christian and non-Christian doctrines alike) and the integrity of theological reflection. Western preoccupation with sophisticated systems of defense and the Western horror of Communism seem to be so disproportionate in the face of humanity's deeper problems. We simply must not permit ourselves to think that the chief religious and moral issues of today are birth control, divorce, or the involvement of clergy in political affairs. Our greatest moral issues appear in the contrast between the massive expenditures for defense on the part of so many nations and the faces staring out of a refugee camp on the Cambodian border, starving parents and children in Somalia, landless poor in Haiti or Bangladesh. It is not unlike the contrast between the women standing in line at a city water pump in a Bombay slum and the automobiles waiting their turn at a car wash in an American suburb. Such scenes reveal the underlying moral and religious perils of our age.

In the course of the preceding chapters, I have made a number of suggestions about the relationship between being religious and being human. On the one hand, I have proposed, we cannot avoid a confrontation with poverty, both the inner poverty which all of us share as sojourners on the earth and the outer poverty which reminds us of what we look like inside. We cannot escape thinking about poverty because from the depths of their hunger, the poor cry out to the rich with the voice of God to refashion the world with justice and love.

On the other hand, religion is neither a means of coping with the hardness of life's sorrows nor a way of assuaging human guilt with promises of forgiveness. Grace never comes cheaply, although it always comes. One cannot build a spiritual life on Psalm 23—"The Lord is my shepherd, there is nothing I shall want"—and the story of the Prodigal Son. Nor can religion substitute for a few well-placed miracles. To claim that today the Lord heals inward blindness instead of physical blindness merely excuses the inability of contemporary disciples to work signs and wonders. But I don't think that religion suffers because we have not witnessed God splitting the seas, or multiplying loaves of bread, or rescuing the dying, or curing the crippled. Religion means looking for God and finding out that God is still in the process of creating us. This discovery can be joyful and consoling, but just as often it proves gruelling and sweaty. After a testing of faith or a humiliating insight into the stiffness of one's soul, one can feel as unfit for the kingdom of God as Peter after the rooster crowed.

Nevertheless, the first religious word about us must not speak of human sinfulness but of human destiny. In God's sight we are not sinners first and only afterward people whom God loves. The first and final word about human beings is that they have been loved and are destined to be wherever God is. Unless looking for God and contemplating him come naturally to human beings, there will be no eternal life. Heaven exists only if human beings are capable of being drawn outside of themselves into the vision of God.

But at the heart of religion there lies compassion, and compassion is God's gift. The 14th-century German mystic, Meister Eckhart, said in one of his sermons:

> As long as you are more concerned for yourself than you are for people you have never seen, you are wrong, and you cannot have even a momentary insight into the simple core of the soul.

Compassion is a contemplative's virtue. It does not come painlessly, because it comes from having our anger and

133

desire for revenge broken—not by the sight of pitiable weakness, but by looking at the greater strength of the one who suffers unjustly and yet forgives. There is a hand that would lift us to a height from which we might see the Lord's glory, as Moses did. But it is also a hand that breaks, pulling us piece by piece through a needle's eye. As a missionary sister in Thailand remarked, maybe being broken is not so terrible, for that must happen to all of us; but to love the hand that breaks—this may be the hardest thing of all!

We would never willingly submit to God's hand, his formative grace over our lives, unless we trusted him, and learning how to trust God, it seems to me, defines the meaning of religious living. Before bringing these pages to a close, therefore, it would be worth our while to make one further reflection on the nature of religion.

Some men and women manage to tie up the world with pious ideas which do not commit them to anything. This is what is meant by developing an ideology, and it is a far cry from looking at life and the world religiously. The danger of reducing faith to an ideology—sacred doctrines that have no teeth—is a perennial one. There is no point in my calling Jesus "Lord" unless I am ready to follow him. However, there is a religious way to view the world. And while religion should not be divorced from the social and ethical demands of the gospel, neither should religion be equated with doing good. A person can be moral without being religious. Since most of us have only a partial hold on the truth, it frequently happens that we are religious without being consistently moral. The kingdom of God, after all, is proclaimed to sinners.

God deals with us as a teacher works with students. A teacher knows that every pupil will not grasp a lesson at the same time. Some learn fast, others need extra help, study aids, examples and illustrations, and additional homework. A skilled teacher will not be surprised by the unevenness of student ability and comprehension in the classroom, and a careful teacher would never treat a student's problems with understanding or retaining class material by accusing the student of moral negligence.

Portraying God on the model of an educator was one of the earliest and richest Christian insights into the way people experience God. For Origen, the great biblical scholar of the third century, God was so much the teacher that every life experience could be regarded as a lesson in which God instructs us, and should we die before our education is complete—before we have been perfectly instructed by the Word—then we would be assigned to seminars in the next life in order to learn fully about ourselves, the universe, and the creator.

Needless to say, sin is not merely a matter of oversight and slowness in learning. But I tend to agree with Origen (as I understand him) that people would offend God less, the more they really knew and understood him. God saves us by teaching us, which is nothing less than redeeming us from our ignorance about him, and about our real origins and destiny.

The best use of audiovisuals occurs in the gospel of Mark, where Jesus is presented as a teacher patiently trying to open the eyes, ears, and minds of the disciples to his message:

> "Do you still not see or understand? Are your hearts hardened? Do you have eyes but fail to see, and ears but fail to hear? And don't you remember?" (Mk 8:17-18).

This marvelous question from the teacher is raised after the healing of a deaf man and just before the curing of a blind one, yet the disciples to the very end of the gospel story seem unable to get the point. The slow pace of their progress and the persistence of their teacher are quite consoling for me.

I offer these remarks about teaching and learning by

135

way of apology for the fact that sometimes religious people do not grasp, either immediately or even after a long time, all the concrete implications of following Christ. To paraphrase John of the Cross' rendition of an old philosophical axiom: The perfect God comes to imperfect creatures in imperfect ways. It would be a mistake to think that every instance of missing the point, even every instance of moral failure, is a sin pure and simple. Living is more complex than that. Where we are ready to locate sin, God may see only the struggle and temporary resistance of a creature still in the process of being fashioned into the divine image. But if moral progress and religious progress do not necessarily run in parallel tracks, what does it mean to view the world religiously? How can we judge whether or not religion is working?

The main business of religion consists in helping people to experience God. Religion is not a matter of learning how to think about God, but of actually experiencing him. God lies at the center of everything, and every created thing centers itself in God. God's presence in creation is not too atomic, so fine that it escapes resolution by the lens of a human eye. The divine presence is too pervasive; it is so intensive that the briefest lapse between our experience of God and our ideas or words about him makes it impossible to be absolutely sure that God has revealed himself and that we have not been tricked by our own imaginings or by the voice of our inner searching. St. Augustine wrote:

> What then, brethren, shall we say of God? For if you have been able to understand what you would like to say, it is not God. If you had been able to comprehend it, you have comprehended something else instead of God. If you have been able to comprehend him as you think, by so thinking you have deceived yourself. This then is not God, if you have comprehended it; but if this is God, then you have not comprehended it. How therefore would you speak of that which you cannot comprehend?

136

Thinking about God, then, is out of the question, since we would have to depend on concepts and images which would always prove too small. But thinking God—and not simply thinking about God—means something else. Thinking God means contemplation; it means contemplating all creatures in the universe and every event of life in terms of their relationship to him who makes all things possible, the centering God, the one in whom all things in the heavens and on the earth hold together. We learn to hear God, to catch God's scent, to notice God's footprint ahead of us. No matter what things in the heavens or on the earth our minds should turn toward, God is there. Furthermore, we come to expect God to be there.

God is not music, not a lover's voice, not a loaf of bread or a pan of rice, not a job failure or a sleepless night, not the birth of a grandchild or the death of a parent. Yet each of these things—music and voices, aromas and fruits, frustrations and distress, laughter and tears—can lift us to the edge of a presence that shimmers before our eyes. Like Moses in the cleft of the rock, we catch a glimpse of the back side of God. And so we feel urged to say thanks for the friend and for the earth's bounty, to say "Why?" in the face of tragedy, or "Let me sleep!" after the distressing night. But to whom do we say this? To what are we talking when such inner feelings escape into words? And once the surge of feeling has fallen into speech, the experience seems to slide away, and we wonder whether we might have been muttering to ourselves.

"What did you go out to the desert to see?" Jesus asked the crowds in reference to John the Baptist. What had they hoped to find in the wilderness? The fact is that we do expect God to be present in barren and out-of-the-way places, in the desert moments of life, in desolation and suffering. Otherwise, we would not be wondering where God is. We would not be demanding to know why he allows innocent people to suffer under heavy poverty and injustice. We would not be so quick to put the universe on trial, or so eager to be set loose from the risks and obligations which religion would impose on us. Unless the crowds had hoped to find a prophet in the desert, a man who could interpret the word of God—for deserts and barren wastes seem to be the favored territory of those driven by the Spirit—they had no reason to seek out John the Baptist. And once they found him—lean, ascetic, burning with God's cause—why did they shrink from his message? If they did not want to be set on fire by his words, they should have stayed at home.

So too with us. If we do not expect the universe, even in its barren and desolate moments, to tell us something about ourselves and the God who is fashioning us, then we should never quit the security of an unexamined life. We ought simply to take for granted every good thing that comes our way and cease complaining about the rest. Of course, God might not permit such an easy detour around the wilderness. God knows that we stand in constant need of a patient but persistent teacher.

It is not my intention to develop an exhaustive account of religious experience, but to point out that religion derives its energy from the human capacity for touching the divine presence. And however beneficial the actions of a religiously converted person might be for human society, it seems to me that religion is not an instrument of social change or moral action, at least not directly. Indeed, our activity, our planning, our way of regarding the world, cannot help but be affected by our contact with God. But we reach out to God for God's own sake. The Word educates us about our inner poverty in order that we might turn poor for the love of God. If turning poor accomplished nothing else except to cultivate resentment toward the universe or feelings of guilt for our limitations and sinfulness, then the Word will have failed us. In other words, God is not a tool for social or moral change. If religion settles for encouraging moral reform, however laudable the objective, then religion will have cheated people of their chance to wrestle with the liv-, ing God and to receive his blessing.

It is possible for men and women to think God, a God who is more truly thought than expressed, and who exists more truly than he is thought, as Augustine put it. God is neither limited in his ways of access into our hearts, nor does God have to wait until our moral life is in order before drawing us to notice his love. Religion is at work when people are willing to risk the wilderness in search of a light which can illumine their darkness. Religion happens when men and women experience the confidence which comes from contemplating God.

Thinking about God, however, is not religion. In the long moments of a quiet, solitary evening, when drawing deep thoughts about the meaning of life keeps pace with the twilight's plunge into darkness, the mind falls easily into thoughts about God. But after a while, I have found, thinking about God tires the mind and dulls my appetite for spiritual things. When philosophers reflect on the existence or nature of God, their writing generally becomes inconclusive, abstract, and disappointing because their thinking rarely reaches God. Thinking about God more often than not turns into a meditation on the universe. One philosophizes about the nature of matter, the eternity or finiteness of time and space, the nature of selfhood, and the possibility of spiritual being. And so you have cosmology, anthropology, psychology, or metaphysics; but religion is none of these. Every aspect of the material universe can be pondered without borrowing a notion of God or divine providence.

Most of us have not been trained to think critically about great philosophical questions: Did the universe have a beginning, or could matter be eternal? What is a spiritual being, and why would a spiritual and perfect God want to create a material and imperfect universe? Is the soul immortal and, if so, can it survive without a body? What is truth, and why is truth of concern to us? We may puzzle over questions like these, but whether by trained minds or by amateurs, speculative attempts to figure out the notion of God or to determine his existence are bound to fail. Why? Because if God does not exist, no amount of thinking will ever uncover that fact. And if God does exist, human thinking is incapable of comprehending why he must. In short, the material universe does not answer some of our most pressing questions about God. With all its galaxies, planets, life forms, and interstellar distances, the universe seems to be theologically neutral.

Modern philosopher Alfred North Whitehead pointed out that in pondering the existence of God the human mind either denies the world its full measure of reality by making God so real that his pre-eminence eclipses the physical universe, or else the mind reduces the existence of God to a mere idea by overestimating the value of the world. In his *Conversion of Augustine*, Romano Guardini made a similar observation with respect to St. Augustine's notion of God:

> Once the mind has grown accustomed to referring every finite condition back to God and his activity, eternity, meaningful abundance, and so forth, the substantiality of earthly things is threatened. They cease to be real incentives to action and worthwhile objects of human striving. Such enfeebling of the finite is not what the gospels mean by "overcoming the world."

Whitehead himself chose to subject God to metaphysical categories in order to protect the consistency of human experience. If God were to transcend human thinking by not fitting into our conceptual schemes, Whitehead argued, then a scandalized reason would have to inform the heart that its experience of God was simply a misreading of facts.

In my private philosophical moments I appreciate Whitehead's observation and Guardini's warning about

Augustine's theology. For when I think about God, I find that at one moment God must be all-important and beside him nothing else matters. But in the next moment, with my feet planted reassuringly on the earth, images of the material world and its everyday concerns return to my memory and appear most important, while thoughts of God drift like smoke into the cavernous darkness of space. In day-to-day living, my attempts to locate God are often frustrated by preconceptions of how God ought to behave.

Thinking about God wearies the mind because the mind is not actually looking at God; it is pondering the world, and given the physical constraints on our means of acquiring information, many questions about the world may never be answered. But most of our questions about God have to be answered by God himself, and many people either fail to ask him or else don't want to hear his answers. We need to be careful about not confusing the search for more information on the universe with our longing for God. When I admit to myself that my heart is looking for God, my mind is never humiliated. But when I am bewildered and overcome by questions about God, the universe, or my own soul which I cannot answer, then my mind feels defeated and rebellious, and my heart loses its taste for anything spiritual.

Although the universe may be theologically neutral, human life is not. Each of us must decide whether to believe that his or her existence is meaningful and worthwhile by virtue of its being God's gift. The warm moments of human life tend to confirm the soul's impulse to trust the world and to believe in a loving God. If life offered only times of laughter and peace around the family hearth, then human beings could not be expected to do more than be glad and grateful for their years of life and breath, and bow out of the world in peace. The world, having been kind, would owe us nothing further. This seems to have been the disposition of the writer behind the Book of Ecclesiastes:

> Then I realized that it is good and proper for a man to eat and drink, and to find satisfaction in his toilsome labor under the sun during the few days of life God has given him—for this is his lot. Moreover, when God gives any man wealth and possessions, and enables him to enjoy them, to accept his lot and be happy in his work—this is a gift of God. He seldom reflects on the days of his life, because God keeps him occupied with gladness of heart (Eccl 5:18-20).

But the human race knows and endures too many moments of sin, suffering, and oppression of the weak, and these things provoke us into questioning the world's integrity. The experience of evil compels us to think about God. The power of death makes reflection on the nature of justice inevitable. Men and women do not simply make a polite departure from the earth because, once in existence, once alive to the possibilities which our minds envision and our souls hope in, we stake our claim on the universe. Justice haunts us and drives our spirit to meditate on life. This accounts for Job's wanting to take God to court, the God "who has denied me justice" and who refused to sit before the bar of human reason. Even if human misery could be eradicated from the planet, we would still have to come to terms with the past. What shall we say to those who perished in famines, or wasted their strength in slavery, or went to the gallows unjustly condemned, or endured the violence of poverty? From the pages of history their cries will continue to haunt us.

Evil is the ultimate irrationality. It grinds against the mind's sense of fairness and demands that we consider the relation between God and the world religiously, not philosophically. Thus the author of the Book of Job depicted God answering Job, not with a reasoned defense of divine providence, but with a spirited affirmation of majesty and power.

If injustice leads us merely to think about God, then

our intelligence will revolt against him. Human reason will reject the careless inconsistency between our poverty and divine grace, because God decreed them both. How do we reconcile those two sides of God's creative work, life and death, the experience of gift and the experience of loss? God must be addressed and questioned directly, as Job did; one must not let go of God until he has replied, as Jacob proved:

> So Jacob was left alone, and a man wrestled with him till daybreak. When the man saw that he could not overpower him, he touched the socket of Jacob's hip so that his hip was wrenched as he wrestled with the man. Then the man said, "Let me go, for it is daybreak." But Jacob replied, "I will not let you go unless you bless me" (Gn 32:24-26).

And Jacob got his blessing. What a stunning example of a person insisting that God do him justice!

Ah, but it is an example from someone else's life. What story shall we be able to tell? Whether or not we untangle the answers to ultimate questions about matter and energy, or the origins of the universe, makes little spiritual difference. But whether or not we wrestle with the possibilities made available to us by our spirit's power to trust and love makes all the difference in the world. Injustice will remain, frightful to the end, the final doubt as to whether turning poor is worth the effort. Injustice invites us to change the world, to hide our faces against its grotesqueness, or to pretend to a sovereignty that we do not enjoy. No, there is no avoiding the needle's eye; but God himself will help us to pass through it, for nothing is impossible to God.

"You seem lost in thought." The missioner who was sharing the bench as we awaited the bus back home broke into my silence. "Yes," I replied, "and that's not a specially comfortable place to be lost, either." Ahead of us, three sets of arms and legs—two belonging to grown men and the other to a young boy—were straining to push a wagonload of bricks up a slight incline in the road. "Porters," my companion informed me. "They rent a wagon and then hire themselves out to the merchants. There is always a crowd of porters at that corner, waiting for work." He pointed to a busy intersection. "They probably work all morning just to pay back the owner of the wagons." After a few moments' pause, he asked, "What do you think Jesus would have said to them?" "To them?" I was surprised by the question. "I was wondering what Jesus would have said to me."